If God Knows What I Need, Why Should I Pray?

Taking the Religion Out of Praying

If God Knows What I Need, Why Should I Pray?

Taking the Religion
Out of Praying

Kent Crockett

HENDRICKSON
PUBLISHERS

If God Knows What I Need, Why Should I Pray? Taking the Religion Out of Praying

Hendrickson Publishers Marketing, LLC
P. O. Box 3473
Peabody, Massachusetts 01961-3473

ISBN 978-1-61970-737-5

Unless otherwise indicated, Scripture quotations in this book are taken from the New American Standard Bible®, Copyright © 1960, 1962, 1963, 1968, 1971, 1972, 1973, 1975, 1977, 1995 by The Lockman Foundation. Used by permission.

Scripture quotations marked KJV are taken from the King James Version of the Bible.

Scripture quotations marked NLT are taken from the Holy Bible, New Living Translation, copyright © 1996, 2004, 2007 by Tyndale House Foundation. Used by permission of Tyndale House Publishers, Inc., Carol Stream, Illinois 60188. All rights reserved.

Scripture quotations marked NKJV are taken from the New King James Version. Copyright © 1982 by Thomas Nelson, Inc. Used by permission. All rights reserved.

Scripture quotations marked NIV are taken from The Holy Bible, New International Version® NIV®, Copyright © 1973, 1978, 1984, 2011 by Biblica, Inc.™ Used by permission. All rights reserved worldwide.

Scripture quotations marked HCSB are taken from the Holman Christian Standard Bible®, Copyright © 1999, 2000, 2002, 2003, 2009 by Holman Bible Publishers. Used by permission. Holman Christian Standard Bible®, Holman CSB®, and HCSB® are federally registered trademarks of Holman Bible Publishers.

Scripture quotations marked NCV are from the New Century Version®. Copyright © 1987, 1988, 1991 by Word Publishing, a division of Thomas Nelson, Inc. Used by permission. All rights reserved.

Italics in Scripture have been added by the author for emphasis.

Printed in the United States of America

First printing — June 2016

Library of Congress Cataloging-in-Publication Data

Names: Crockett, Kent, 1952- author.
Title: If God knows what I need why should I pray? : taking the religion out
    of praying / Kent Crockett.
Description: Peabody, MA : Hendrickson Publishers, 2016.
Identifiers: LCCN 2016007937 | ISBN 9781619707375 (alk. paper)
Subjects: LCSH: Prayer--Christianity.
Classification: LCC BV210.3 .C755 2016 | DDC 248.3/2--dc23 LC record available at
    http://lccn.loc.gov/2016007937

DEDICATION

To my grandchildren Maddox, Annie, and Hawkins Tate,
and to all my descendants yet to be born.

"He commanded our fathers that they should teach them
to their children, that the generation to come might
know, even the children yet to be born, that they may
arise and tell them to their children, that they should
put their confidence in God and not forget the works of
God, but keep His commandments." (Psalm 78:5–7)

CONTENTS

PART 2: ANSWERS TO QUESTIONS

PART 3: PRAYING SPECIFIC REQUESTS

FOREWORD

Do we really need *another* book on prayer? Yes, if that book addresses issues that aren't mentioned in the many other writings on this subject. If praying is a dreaded duty for you or if you aren't seeing worthwhile results, this book will challenge you to reexamine how you pray.

Before you can pray correctly, you must first realize that you might be praying incorrectly, and then make the needed adjustments. The Pharisees prayed for hours each day and never touched God's heart. Could you have fallen into the same trap? The people of that day had learned how to pray from the Pharisees, so Jesus spent much of His ministry trying to get the people to *unlearn* what they had been wrongly taught.

If God Knows What I Need, Why Should I Pray? will give you insights into how prayer works. It's critical that you grasp the four purposes of prayer because having this knowledge will inspire you to bring your requests to God.

Do you understand that some things will not happen in your life unless you pray? Otherwise, prayer serves no purpose. The Bible says you do not have because you do not ask.

Do you realize that when you pray the earthly realm reaches into the spiritual realm?

Do you fully understand what it means to pray in the name of Jesus?

Before reading this book, I ask you to lay aside your preconceived notions about prayer. You cannot learn anything unless you're open to ideas that you've never considered before. Kent Crockett allows the Scripture to speak for itself. It's my prayer that you will be enlightened and discover the freedom and joy you'll experience through dialoging with the living God.

Peter Lord
Author of *The 2959 Plan*
and *Hearing God*

ACKNOWLEDGMENTS

I would like to give special thanks to the following people:

My precious wife, Cindy. You've been my wife, best friend, mother of our children, Mimi to our grandchildren, my personal editor, and the one who has loved me at all times. I thank God every day that He gave you to me.

Peter Lord, Ron and Cindy Harwell, Paul and Debby Baskin, John and Donnie Mitchell, Lonnie and Darlene Brand, Tom and Bev Ovesen, Randy and Jane Abele, Mike and Cat Baxter, Bruce and Virginia Crockett, Will Fisch, Jim Elsey, Teresa Mackender, Sterling Myers, Sam and Ruby Doyle, Pete and Robin Shultis, and Sean and Liz Ezell, who have been a great encouragement to me.

My agent, Les Stobbe. Thank you for your wisdom and for representing me in an ever-changing publishing world.

Patricia Anders, Hannah Brown, and the entire team at Hendrickson Publishers for the wonderful work you do to further God's kingdom.

PART 1

HOW PRAYER WORKS

1 | WHAT IF WE'VE BEEN DOING IT ALL WRONG?

> "You are mistaken, not understanding the
> Scriptures nor the power of God." (Matthew 22:29)

Which best describes your prayer life?

- I love praying and I see God answering my prayers. (If so, you're on the right track.)

- I hate praying because it's so boring.

- Praying makes absolutely no difference in my life.

- I don't understand why I need to pray.

- The only reason I pray is to keep God from getting mad at me.

If you checked any answer but the first one, you've just identified how I once thought about praying. And if we're honest, most people feel like I did about prayer. But maybe there's another reason why it's not working for so many of us. Perhaps we've just been doing it wrong.

A journalist assigned to the Jerusalem bureau rented an apartment that overlooked the Wailing Wall, which is a holy site where Jews pray. Every day when she looked out the window, she noticed an elderly Jewish man praying at the Wall.

Curiosity got the best of her. She grabbed her pen and notebook, rushed over to the Wailing Wall and introduced herself to the old man.

"I'm a journalist and I've noticed you come here every day to pray. How long have you done this, and what are you praying for?"

"I've come here every day for twenty-five years," the man replied. "In the morning I pray for world peace and the brotherhood of man. Then I go home, have a cup of tea, and come back here and pray for the eradication of all disease from the face of the earth."

"That's amazing!" the journalist exclaimed as she scribbled down notes. "How does it make you feel to come here every day and pray for these things?"

The old man closed his eyes and sighed, "It's like talking to a wall."

For so many people, prayer is like talking to a wall. If that's the case with you, then it won't be long before you quit doing it.

Is it possible that we've somehow missed what God intended prayer to be? What if it doesn't matter to God whether we pray with our eyes open instead of closed? Could it be that He might *not* want us to pray publicly in restaurants? Many people only pray in church, but what if most of our praying should be happening when we're *not* at church? And what if something even more fundamental about our attitude needs to change? Could we be doing it all wrong? It wouldn't be first time that "religious" people got off track.

Getting It Wrong, Part 1

The book of Malachi describes how worship in Israel had deteriorated from a glorious celebration to a wearisome obligation. Thousands of worshippers came to the temple to give their offerings to the priests to sacrifice to the Lord. But instead of bringing the best of their flocks to honor God, they brought diseased animals that weren't fit to eat. The priests accepted them anyway, presuming that God wouldn't know the difference. They ignored the command in Deuteronomy 17:1 that prohibited the offering of defective animals.

Neither the priests nor the people ever worshipped joyfully. Instead, they were always complaining, "How tiresome it is!" (Malachi 1:13). (Have you ever said that about going to church?) They didn't believe God could see their pathetic offerings or hear their whining. *Not a single person in the entire crowd had a clue that God was screaming from heaven for them to stop.* You'd think that just one person could hear the Lord say:

> "Oh that there were one among you who would shut the gates, that you might not uselessly kindle fire on My altar! I am not pleased with you," says the LORD of hosts, "nor will I accept an offering from you." (Malachi 1:10)

The Lord was so upset by their disgusting offerings that He pleaded for someone—anyone—to have the guts to lock the gates of the temple. He wanted some brave soul to step up to the plate and stop everyone from entering the door and bringing in even more diseased animals that He refused to accept.

Place yourself in this story and imagine for a moment that you are that courageous person who responds to God's request. You single-handedly overpower the guards and lock the gates. You choose to be an unpopular one-person army who shuts down the entire worship center in Israel!

Even though *you are the only one obeying God*, it appears to everyone else in Israel that you are an evil troublemaker for trying to stop their worship services. You're banished from the temple for the rest of your life and branded as a heretic.

At the time, not a single person heard what God was saying through Malachi. All these people were going through the motions of worship, yet they were doing it all wrong. Presenting their offerings had become a dull, bothersome task. The passion in their hearts had died long ago but the rituals continued. The altar that was meant to be used for acts of worshipping the living God became an incinerator for burning their garbage. They carried on business as usual, oblivious to the fact that the Lord in heaven wanted them to stop their meaningless religious activities.

How did their worship degenerate to such a low state when everyone truly thought they were pleasing God? Their hearts drifted away from Him—and it happened so gradually no one even noticed.

GETTING IT WRONG, PART 2

Fast forward approximately five hundred years. It's the same temple, but this time Jesus really did shut down the false worship. By then the worshippers had turned the temple into a profitable business, and just as in the book of Malachi, they never realized they were doing anything wrong.

> They came to Jerusalem. And He entered the temple and began to cast out those who were buying and selling in the temple, and overturned the tables of the moneychangers and the seats of those who were selling doves; and *He would not permit anyone to carry goods through the temple*. And He began to teach and say to them, "Is it not written, 'My house shall be called *a house of prayer* for all the nations'? But you have made it a robbers' den." (Mark 11:15–17)

How did worship turn into retail sales? Didn't any of these people read the book of Malachi? Of course they did. They simply believed the message applied only to those people "back then." They weren't bringing defective animals to sacrifice the way their forefathers did, so they assumed everything was just fine. But it wasn't. They got it all wrong—again!

Merchants brought their best animals to sell to those who came from long distances to worship and couldn't bring a sacrifice of their own. They charged high fees for this service. Temple tax collectors set up shop to receive a half shekel from every Israelite over the age of twenty, which brought in an enormous amount of revenue (see Exodus 30:13–15). People from other countries needed to exchange their foreign money for acceptable temple currency, so moneychangers were authorized to charge them a fee for each transaction. The temple had turned into a huge stockyard and banking institution, filled with people standing in lines to conduct financial transactions.

Jesus said they had turned the temple into a "robbers' den," which was a hideaway or cave where thieves would escape and split up their loot. No doubt the moneychangers and merchants who could be seen huddled together and counting their money looked exactly like thieves dividing up their stolen goods. With so many animals to be sold and money to be made, everyone had forgotten about the real reason they were there.

Is it possible that some of our modern-day church services have also fallen into this same trap?

GETTING IT WRONG, PART 3

In Jesus' day, a new group of religious leaders was in charge in Israel: the Pharisees. No one was more dedicated to prayer than the Pharisees. They diligently prayed for hours on end, although they never made contact with God. Jesus quoted Isaiah's prophecy to them, "This people honors Me with their lips, but their heart is far away from Me" (Matthew 15:8). With God, the feeling was mutual. He didn't talk to them either (see John 5:37).

What a shocking revelation, considering how often these guys feigned conversation with God. They deliberately set aside times for prayer at 9 a.m., noon, and 3 p.m., praying an hour each time. Every morning and evening they prayed the Shema, which had to be spoken before 9 a.m. and in the evening before 9 p.m. Where were these specific instructions on prayer found in the Scriptures?

Nowhere. Some Pharisee made it up.

Now envision hundreds of Pharisees bellowing longwinded prayers on the street corners and in the marketplace for everyone to hear. It must have been most impressive—and made those who weren't as committed to praying feel extremely guilty. I'm sure many of the passersby thought, *I need to pray more, like those Pharisees.*

In their minds, these religious leaders were the perfect role models because they were so dedicated. If you wanted to know exactly what God was like, all you had to do was take a look at a pious Pharisee saying his long prayers. Who could ever doubt that these men were the closest people to God on the entire planet?

Here's a shocking thought. *That wasn't the way they were supposed to pray.* This charade would have continued if Jesus had not shown up to contradict everything these bogus religious leaders had taught people about God. He unapologetically announced, "You are of your father the devil, and you want to do the desires of your father" (John 8:44). He boldly proclaimed that the Pharisees were not from God at all and *they had learned how to pray from Satan himself.* The devil taught them to pray incorrectly—and to teach others to follow their example.

No Pharisee had ever taught them to pray in a closet.

We never see Jesus standing on a street corner with a bullhorn, belting out flowery recitations to impress the shoppers in the marketplace. Instead, He taught just the opposite of the traditions imposed by the Pharisees. He said, "When you pray, go into your inner room, and when you have shut the door, pray to your Father who is in secret" (Matthew 6:6). The inner room was a tiny closet used for storage. No one, except for God, would be able to see the person praying.

Can't you picture His audience looking at each other in disbelief? No Pharisee had ever taught them to pray in a closet. They were instructed to pray loudly and publicly on the street corners, so that bystanders would observe their fictitious commitment to God. Praying privately was a radical new teaching that contradicted everything they had learned about prayer. The Pharisees taught that prayers were to be said where crowds gathered—on street corners, in synagogues, and at the temple. In their minds, praying in public would set a good example for the less spiritual. But Jesus just stuck a pin in that balloon.

GETTING IT WRONG, PART 4?

I'm not accusing you of praying incorrectly. I don't even know you. Perhaps you love spending time communicating with God and most of your prayers are being answered. If so, you're on the right track. But you are in the minority. Most people can go through the entire day without talking to God for even a minute. For others, prayer only occurs during a worship service.

I will confess to you that I spent too many years getting prayer wrong. When I began my quest to become a follower of Jesus Christ it never occurred to me that Satan would try to sidetrack me. But if the devil couldn't stop me from doing what was right, he would try to trick me into doing the right thing in the wrong way. He wanted prayer to become a useless ritual where I would say pious words without my heart ever connecting with the Lord. As long as I was praying wrongly, it would keep me from genuinely connecting with God in prayer.

In my earlier years, I was taught that I was not a committed Christian unless I prayed for an hour a day. The earlier in the morning I did this, the better. This plan might work fine for some people, but it didn't work for me. It was hard for me to get through the hour without repeating myself and I found myself constantly glancing at the clock to see how much time I had left. Whenever I did pray for an hour, my heart swelled with pride and I would subtly mention my prayer time to others. It didn't occur to me that this was exactly what the Pharisees did.

On days when I didn't put in my full hour, I felt like I had failed God and assumed He was upset with me. I finally reached a point where I detested hearing the word *prayer*. No one ever explained to me the real reasons why I needed to pray.

You will get prayer wrong just the way I did if you:

- Secretly want others to see you praying

- Pray only when you are in a church service

- Say words without connecting your heart with God

- Believe that the longer your prayers are, the more they will impress God

- Think of prayer as a tiresome ritual

- Only pray when you want something from God

- Primarily request things for selfish reasons

- Think the only correct way to pray is to bow your head, close your eyes, and talk out loud

- Don't really believe God hears your prayers and will answer

If thousands of worshippers in the book of Malachi hated bringing their offerings to God, it's also possible for us to detest praying. If the Pharisees could pray for hours and never touch God's heart, it's possible for us to do the same.

The devil loves for us to pray in the wrong way—unenthusiastically following rituals, praying so we will look spiritual, and asking only with selfish motives. For every spiritual activity God wants us to do, Satan has a counterfeit way that looks nearly identical to the real thing.

Eventually I learned something was terribly wrong with the way I was praying. Maybe you've felt the same way. In this book I will share a few things I've learned that I hope will liberate you into having a joyful relationship with God. Understanding the four purposes of prayer is the place to begin.

> For every spiritual activity God wants us to do, Satan has a counterfeit way that looks nearly identical to the real thing.

2 | THE FOUR PURPOSES OF PRAYER

> "The earnest prayer of a righteous
> person has great power and produces
> wonderful results." (James 5:16 NLT)

Chimpanzees have been taught how to use sign language to communicate what they want. In his book *The Language Instinct*, Steven Pinker talks about a chimp named Nim that learned how to sign. Can you figure out what Nim was asking in this message?

> *"Nim eat. Nim eat. Banana me me me eat. You me banana me banana you. Banana me, me eat. You me banana, me banana you."*

Or what about this message?

> *"Give orange me give eat orange me eat orange give me eat orange give me you."*

You don't have to be a zoologist to figure that one out.

Suppose that chimps could be taught to pray to God. What would their prayers be like? Two things stand out from Nim's messages. First, Nim tends to repeat the same words over and over. Second, every message concerns something Nim wants. From these two characteristics, we can assume that chimp prayers would be repetitive, self-centered, and demanding.[1] Come to think of it, that's how most humans pray!

Jesus said, "When you are praying, do not use meaningless repetition as the Gentiles do, for they suppose that they will be heard for their many words" (Matthew 6:7). The heathens tried to wear out their gods with endless babbling, and the Pharisees also prayed for hours on end, thinking they were impressing God. They were saying monkey prayers, mindlessly repeating the same words over and over but never understanding the real purpose of prayer. Even the Lord's Prayer can become a meaningless repetition if we recite it with our hearts disengaged from God.

Many people think the purpose of prayer is to inform God about what they need. But that cannot be the reason for prayer, because Jesus said, "Your Father knows what you need before you ask Him" (Matthew 6:8). He already knows. So if God already knows what I need, why should I pray?

Years ago when I was confused about how to pray, I was like the little boy who wrote down his prayer requests and posted them on the ceiling over his bed. Instead of saying his prayers every night, he crawled into bed and pointed at the note. Since God already knew, why bother to say them?

One of the first things new believers should be taught is how prayer works and why we need to pray. I remember being told that I should pray, but not one person ever explained to me *why* I should pray. Understanding the reason why we're doing any task is vital for keeping us motivated.

Suppose I said to you, "I'd like you to do me a favor. I want you to dig some six-foot-deep holes in my backyard."

You raise an eyebrow. "You want me to do *what*? That sounds really weird. Why do you want me to do that?"

"It doesn't matter. I need the holes dug and I want you to do it."

You make up an excuse why you can't do it. Then you start feeling guilty about not helping, so you reluctantly give in to my request. Fifteen minutes into the project your back starts hurting. You keep glancing at your watch, wondering how much longer you will have to dig holes.

Most people pray like that—reluctantly digging holes without understanding why. We'll do it, but only because we feel obligated. We will go through the ritual of prayer just to get it over with and scratch it off our religious to-do list.

Now consider a different scenario. This time I explain to you why I'm asking you to dig. "I found out that my great-grandfather buried a treasure chest that's worth a fortune in my backyard. Since you're my best friend, I'll give you half the treasure if you'll do the digging. Don't get discouraged if you don't find it at first. Keep digging until you find it. Half the treasure is yours, but only if you'll dig it up."

Now because you understand the reason I want you to dig, you're suddenly excited and have completely forgotten about your backache. In your mind, you're not digging holes anymore. You're searching for hidden treasure. You're energized because of my promise that you'll be rewarded for your work.

Once the light bulb comes on in your mind that God will reveal himself to you in prayer, open doors of opportunity, and bless your life in a better way, you'll always be excited about praying. You'll see that praying isn't a duty but a privilege.

FOUR REASONS TO PRAY

I'll admit that I don't understand everything about how prayer works. No one does. How is it that I can talk with God about an issue and in some mysterious way, the prayer changes my destiny? Whether or not you understand how prayer works, conversing with God can change your heart and your circumstances. If you want to look forward to communicating with your heavenly Father, it's essential that you understand prayer's four purposes.

PURPOSE 1. PRAYER IS HOW YOU DIALOGUE AND FELLOWSHIP WITH GOD.

God could have said, "There's no such thing as prayer. It doesn't exist. You're not allowed to talk to me, and even if you try, I won't listen to you. I refuse to help you if you're in trouble. Need to know the right path to take? Tough luck, you're on your own. If you need assistance, I'm sorry, but you don't have a prayer."

Imagine going your entire life without being able to talk to God. But if you don't pray, it's the same as if there were no such thing as prayer. Instead of abandoning you to your own fate, God gave you the privilege of prayer. A privilege means something you *get to* do rather than you've *got to* do.

Prayer is connecting your heart to God's heart. The Pharisees said prayers for hours each day, but they never connected with Him. They never truly acknowledged His presence. Jesus said they honored God with their lips but their hearts were far away (Matthew 15:8). The Lord wants you to humbly come before Him and honestly share everything that's on your heart. "Trust in Him at all times. Pour out your heart before Him" (Psalm 62:8).

> Prayer is connecting your
> heart to God's heart.

It's vital that you believe that He hears you when you pray. "This is the confidence which we have before Him, that, if we ask anything according to His will, He hears us. And *if we know that He hears us* in whatever we ask, we know that we have the requests which we have asked from Him" (1 John 5:14–15). If you don't believe that God is listening to you, it will be like talking to a wall. Why would you want to pray if you didn't believe He was hearing what you were saying?

Prayer isn't just talking to Him, but also listening to Him speak to you. He's the living God who wants to communicate with all His children. It's through prayer that the Holy Spirit will speak to you, guide you, and give you wisdom. In upcoming chapters we'll talk about how He does this.

Purpose 2. Prayer is how you participate in His will being done on earth.

God could have done everything for you by Himself, but instead He instituted prayer so that you can be a co-laborer with Him. He offers you the opportunity to participate in accomplishing His purposes on earth through praying. Jesus taught us to pray to the heavenly Father, "Your will be done on earth as it is in heaven" (Matthew 6:10). Prayer can actually cause things to happen on earth *that wouldn't happen otherwise*, which explains why it's such a magnificent privilege.

Someone has said praying is like giving God permission to do what He already wants to do. It's probably more accurate to say that prayer is God giving you permission—to give Him permission. This doesn't mean God is obeying you, given that He is the one who gave you the privilege of prayer and designed it to work in this way. He wants you to call out to Him to intervene in your situation when you need help.

Prayer is a valuable privilege the Lord has granted to His children to change their destinies. How often you want to use the privilege is up to you. God is waiting for you to RSVP—Respond to the Sacred, Valuable Privilege.

Prayer is like a passkey that can open doors for you. It won't open every door but it will unlock the doors that are in God's will. You can choose to use the key or not to use it. But if you don't use the key, the doors that could have been opened might remain closed.

Some things will not happen in your life unless you pray. After all, if your prayers didn't make any difference, then what would be the use of praying? God sometimes puts natural limits on what He will do, but if you'll pray He will expand those limits. He withholds some blessings because you haven't asked for them. He says, "You do not have because you do not ask" (James 4:2).

In the Old Testament, we read how Sennacherib, the king of Assyria, threatened to conquer the land of Judah. Hezekiah, the king of Judah, knew he would be defeated unless God intervened. He entered the temple and asked the Lord for help.

Some things will not happen in
your life unless you pray.

God told Hezekiah, "*Because you have prayed to Me* about Sennacherib king of Assyria, I have heard you" (2 Kings 19:20). The Lord caused Sennacherib to hear a rumor and return to his own land, where he was killed (2 Kings 19:7, 36–37). Jerusalem was delivered from destruction because of Hezekiah's prayer. But what would have happened if he had not prayed? Sennacherib probably would have conquered Jerusalem.

King Hezekiah used the passkey to bring about God's will on earth. Although the Lord is sovereign and can do whatever He wants, He places the key in your hand that can change your situation for the better. But it's up to you to put the key into the lock and unlock the door.

Your prayers can bring about salvation, wisdom, provision, protection, guidance, and positive change in others, which will be discussed in more detail later. Here are a few things that can come to pass as a result of prayer.

- *Provision.* "All things for which you pray and ask, believe that you have received them, and they shall be granted you" (Mark 11:24).

- *Protection.* "Keep watching and praying, that you may not come into temptation" (Mark 14:38).

- *Strength.* "But keep on the alert at all times, praying in order that you may have strength to escape all these things that are about to take place" (Luke 21:36).

- *Opportunity.* ". . . praying at the same time for us as well, that God may open up to us a door for the word" (Colossians 4:3).

- *Conviction.* "Pray for those who mistreat you" (Luke 6:28).

- *Guidance.* "If any of you lack wisdom let him ask of God" (James 1:5).

- *Comfort.* "Is anyone among you suffering? Let him pray" (James 5:13).

- *Healing.* "Pray for one another, so that you may be healed" (James 5:16).

PURPOSE 3. PRAYER PROVES TO GOD HOW DESPERATELY YOU WANT SOMETHING.

Jesus said, "Your Father knows what you need before you ask Him" (Matthew 6:8). He didn't say "Your Father knows you *don't* need things so *don't* ask." Since our Father knows you need certain things, it's not selfish to ask Him to supply what's necessary to live. And when He answers your prayer, you experience His great love for you in a tangible way.

You are most passionate about those things you persistently mention in your prayers. When you pray out of desperation, you catch God's ear because you're showing Him that you trust Him with the things you care most about. The desperate cries of your heart can actually move the Father's heart. When Lazarus died his sister Mary came crying to Jesus. "When Jesus therefore saw her weeping, and the Jews who came with her, also weeping, *He was deeply moved in spirit* and was troubled" (John 11:33). Mary's heart touched Jesus' heart. Immediately after this He raised Lazarus from the dead.

On another occasion, Jesus was leaving Jericho when He heard someone urgently calling for help. Even though many people were making requests, Jesus heard the pleas of a blind beggar named Bartimaeus who sat by the road. When people told the beggar to keep quiet, *he shouted even louder*, "Son of David, have mercy on me!" (Mark 10:48). Out of all the voices requesting help, Bartimaeus caught Jesus' attention above the rest because he was the most desperate.

Jesus stopped and asked, "What do you want Me to do for you?" (Mark 10:51).

Wasn't it obvious? A blind man is crying out for help but Jesus doesn't know what he wants? Of course He knew. Remember, the purpose of prayer is not to inform God about what He already knows. Jesus knew the blind man desired to be healed, but He wanted to hear this sightless man verbally express his specific request.

Bartimaeus could have asked for a seeing eye dog or a white cane. Instead, this blind beggar said, "I want to receive my sight!" Opening the eyes of a blind person was a miracle that had never occurred in the Old Testament. The Jews believed that the Messiah would be identified if He was able to give sight to the blind (see Isaiah 29:18, 35:5, 42:7). Bartimaeus asked Jesus to give him sight because he knew He must be the Messiah. He had never seen Jesus but trusted Him enough to ask for a miracle that had never occurred before. And he got it! It might not have happened if he hadn't called out to Him in sheer desperation. Jesus hearing his request played an important role in his prayer being answered.

Desperation is an important element of prayer because it shows how badly you want something. If you don't care, you won't pray. But if something is important to you, you'll be persistent and will keep expressing your request to the Lord. Obviously, not every prayer is said with the same seriousness and intensity. Prayers of desperation are filled with passion and determination that touch God's heart. The Lord designed prayer to work in partnership with Him, where we have a role to fulfill. He wants us to call out to Him with persistent faith because "the effective, fervent prayer of a righteous man avails much" (James 5:16 NKJV).

Another way you can prove to God the seriousness of your request is through fasting, which means not eating, or giving up certain foods, while you are seeking God. When you add fasting to your prayer request, it demonstrates that you're so desperate for the answer to come that you are willing to go without eating.

PURPOSE 4. PRAYER IS HOW YOU RELEASE YOUR BURDENS TO GOD.

"Be anxious for nothing, but in everything by prayer and supplication with thanksgiving let your requests be made known to God. And the peace of God, which surpasses all comprehension, shall guard your hearts and your minds in Christ Jesus" (Philippians 4:6–7).

Jesus described His followers as sheep (John 10:27) and God didn't design sheep to carry heavy loads. Pack mules carry baggage, but you've never seen sheep carrying baggage on their backs. When you're burdened down and stressed out, the Lord wants you to release all your "baggage" to Him through prayer.

A man was going through a difficult time and went to his pastor for advice. The pastor asked, "Have you released your situation into the Lord's hands?"

"Oh yes. Many times," the man answered.

"You can't give something to the Lord many times," the minister replied, "unless you've taken it back many times. Take your burden to Him and leave it there."

Jerry was walking to the laundromat carrying his dirty clothes in a duffel bag on his back. On the way, he ran into his friend Lou who told him about all the problems he was going through.

"Lou, why don't you pray and give everything that bothers you to the Lord?" Jerry asked.

"I've already done that, but I'm still burdened down. How can I know for sure that I've really handed my problems to God?"

Jerry let go of his duffel bag, which fell off his back to the ground.

"How do I know that I dropped the sack? I haven't looked around to see if it's off my back."

"You know because you let go of it and it isn't weighing you down anymore."

"And that's how you'll know if you've released your problems to God. They won't weigh you down anymore."

Praying means transferring your concerns into the Father's hands. "Casting all your care on Him because He cares for you" (1 Peter 5:7 HCSB). True prayer means letting go of your problem, placing it in the Lord's hands, and trusting Him to take care of it.

When you throw a ball to someone, you first have to let go of it. You release your problems by letting go of them and giving them to God. It's natural to feel stressed out and burdened down by various trials. And if the circumstances don't change, you might feel like the weight of the problem is getting even heavier. Worrying won't do anything to fix your problem. But prayer really does work. If you're still burdened down after you've prayed, you can learn to let go by realizing that God can be trusted to carry your burdens for you.

Now that you understand the four purposes of prayer, you can start using the passkey to unlock God's blessings. But to pray effectively, you might need to make some adjustments to your concept of God. Your faith will grow once you have a correct understanding of His power and character.

3 | YOUR CONCEPT OF GOD DETERMINES YOUR FAITH

> "It shall be done to you according to
> your faith." (Matthew 19:29)

Do you believe that a NBA pro basketball player can jump high enough to dunk a basketball? You're probably saying "yes" because his athletic ability makes it an easy task.

But do you believe that the author of this book can dunk a basketball? I'll give you a hint. I'm 5´9˝ and my jumping ability is limited. I can already hear your answer. You don't believe I can do it. But I really can dunk a basketball—if someone will lower the net for me.

In this illustration the height of the basketball net represents the size of your problem, and the answer to your prayer is like God dunking the ball. Your faith will determine how you see your problems—and how you view God.

When you are faced with a difficulty, it's normal to wonder if God can help you get through it. If you believe He is all-powerful, it doesn't matter how high the net is set because you have faith that He can solve any problem. But if you believe that the Lord has limited abilities, your lack of faith will force you to lower the net and you'll assume that He can only fix small problems.

Your faith is determined by your concept of God. We typically allow the size of our problem to define God's ability to help us. It should be the other way around. The way to increase your faith is to believe what God has revealed through the Scriptures about His unlimited power.

When Erasmus debated with Martin Luther in the sixteenth century, Luther told him, "Your thoughts of God are too human." Let's be honest. Most people have adopted a humanized concept of God. We've created a false god in our minds who is feeble and uncaring, and then we live in response to that untrue imagination. To correct our misconception, we must realize that the god in our minds isn't anything like who the Almighty God really is.

WRONG CONCEPT 1—A GOD WITH HUMAN ABILITIES

Since it's difficult for us to grasp the impossible, we squeeze God into our little box of logic so we can better understand Him. This god-in-a-box can only do what we believe is humanly possible. Then whenever we encounter a trial, we have no faith that He will come through for us. We see His ability the same way we see our own ability as helpless human beings.

Some people have even formed a whole theology based on the idea that God doesn't do miracles anymore, which lowers the goalpost. However, Jesus' statement is still true: "With people this is impossible, but with God all things are possible" (Matthew 19:26). Scripture warns us about listening to those "having a form of godliness *but denying its power*. Have nothing to do with such people" (2 Timothy 3:5). God doesn't want their unbelief to infect our faith.

One reason Jesus came to earth was to correct our wrong ideas about God and to reveal who He actually is. Some people living in that day believed God was like a judgmental Pharisee who enforced a legalistic book of rules. Others followed the intellectual Sadducees, who didn't believe that God could do miracles or that anything supernatural could happen. The first thing Jesus wanted to do was to destroy these false concepts of God. "The Son of God appeared for this purpose, that He might destroy the works of the devil" (1 John 3:8).

To accomplish this, Jesus used *shock treatments*—mind-boggling stories that jolted people out of thinking like humans so they would start thinking like God, "so that [their] faith might not rest on human wisdom, but *on God's power*" (1 Corinthians 2:5). He stunned everyone when He said, "Truly I say to you, whoever says to this mountain, 'Be taken up and cast into the sea,' and does not doubt in his heart, but believes that what he says is going to happen, it will be granted him" (Mark 11:23).

> Jesus used *shock treatments*—
> mind-boggling stories that jolted
> people out of thinking like humans so
> they would start thinking like God.

Imagine seeing a huge mountain rising out of the ground, hovering in mid-air and then zooming miles away into an ocean. His statement was so astonishing and absurd that if Christ Himself had not spoken these words, it certainly would not have been recorded in God's Word.

But it is. And just to make sure no one would tamper with His statement by trying to make it merely symbolic, Jesus said, "*Truly* I say to you" because He wanted to reinforce that mountain-casting is truly possible. Grasping this one truth about God's ability to do what's physically impossible will increase our faith to biblical proportions.

Why would anyone want to transplant a mountain to another place? Moving a mountain into the sea serves no practical purpose, unless you are plugging a huge hole at the bottom of the ocean. As far as we know, no one has ever used their faith to cast a mountain, or even a molehill for that matter, into a large body of water. Not even Jesus attempted to do this, but that doesn't negate the validity of His claim.

Why did Jesus pick such a bizarre example of what faith can do?

Because logic only thinks inside the box, and He had to shock us so we would think outside the box. Faith is thinking the way God thinks. He wants us to understand the incredible power of faith, so He chose an example that we would never consider—something that's totally out of the realm of human possibility. He said this to increase our faith in His ability, which will raise the bar for us when it comes to answered prayer.

Faith is thinking the way God thinks.

Jesus could have given the disciples a visual demonstration by speaking to the Mount of Olives and commanding it to uproot. We can imagine what a scene this would have caused. While everyone is gawking at the mountain floating above them, He points to the southeast and orders it to fly several miles away to the Dead Sea. As soon as the mountain is hovering in the correct position, He orders it to drop, creating a splash heard round the world. That certainly would have added an exclamation point to the end of His sermon.

Jesus didn't need to exhibit this incredible feat because He had already given them a visual demonstration on the previous day. He had cursed a fig tree saying that no one would ever eat from it again. He didn't curse it because He had a grudge against fig trees or was in a bad mood that day. He was conducting a faith experiment for His students to observe.

Although the tree didn't have ears to hear His words, it obeyed His voice and withered up (see Mark 11:13–14, 20–21). His power-filled words directed at a figless tree showed them what faith in Him can do.

Jesus told us to "Have faith in God" (Mark 11:22). He didn't instruct us to have faith *in faith*. He wants us to place our eyes of faith on the God who can do the impossible. It's not a matter of how great our faith is. It's how great our God is.

It doesn't matter if it's a fig tree or a mountain. The same God who can shrivel up a tree can also cast a mountain into the sea. And the same Lord who can move a mountain is more than able to solve any problem.

WRONG CONCEPT 2—A GOD WHO WANTS PEOPLE TO SUFFER

Some people have a totally twisted idea concerning God's nature. If you grew up being abused by the people who cared for you, or were raised without any true caregivers, it may be a big challenge for you to grasp the concept of a loving heavenly Father. Yes, you can receive a healthy view of God, but first you might have to destroy the false concept in your mind of an abusive, angry father who only wants to punish you.

Jesus told the Pharisees, "You are of your father the devil, and you want to do the desires of your father" (John 8:44). He was accusing these false teachers of receiving their wrong concept of God from their evil spiritual father, Satan. If you had an abusive father or caregiver, that person's evil actions were not like God's. Don't confuse the two spiritual "fathers" that Jesus talks about—the devil and our true Father, God. No matter what your past, it's important that you receive your concept of God from Him alone.

Christ once told a parable about a master who gave talents (which were bags of money) to his three slaves to manage while he was away on a journey (Matthew 25:14–30). The first two slaves went out and used their money to make profits for their master. But the third slave buried his bag of money in the ground and did nothing with it.

When the master returned from his journey, the three slaves had to give him a report about what they had done. The first two slaves reported that they had doubled his money. Their boss praised them for their faithful work and rewarded them accordingly.

But when the third slave was asked what he had done with his talent, he replied:

"Master, *I knew you to be a hard man*, reaping where you did not sow, and gathering where you scattered no seed. And *I was afraid*, and went away and hid your talent in the ground; see you have what is yours." (Matthew 25:24–25).

In the parable, the master represents God. The third slave didn't produce anything for his boss because he had a distorted view of him. The slave revealed exactly what he thought of him, saying, "I knew you to be *a hard man*." He had an incorrect concept of the character of his boss. He wasn't a hard master. In fact, he was kind and generous. He had graciously rewarded the two other slaves with a promotion.

But the third slave didn't recognize or appreciate his master's generous heart. If he had truly understood that his master was gracious and kind, he wouldn't have been afraid of him or buried his money. He would have acted like the other two slaves, who served their master cheerfully.[2] This parable shows how our concept of God determines whether we love Him or despise Him.

"THE TRUTH WILL MAKE YOU FREE"

Jesus said to the Jews who believed in Him, "If you continue to obey my teaching, you are truly my followers. Then you will know the truth, and the truth will make you free" (John 8:31–32 NCV). The truth by itself doesn't make anyone free. It is *knowing* the truth that makes us free. But the opposite is also true. Believing ideas that are not true keeps us in bondage.

Some people form a wrong belief about God based on tragedies. They conclude that He is responsible for causing them or blame Him for not preventing them. This is why our faith must be based on what God has revealed about himself in the Scriptures. The following verses reveal the true nature of God.

- "He Himself is kind to ungrateful and evil men" (Luke 6:35). God is kind even to those people who hate Him and are always complaining.

- "God is love" (1 John 4:8). Aren't you glad that God's nature is love instead of hate? We would have no hope if the Bible had said "God is hate."

- "Every good thing given and every perfect gift is from above, coming down from the Father of lights" (James 1:17). This verse explains that He gives good things to us and is the exact opposite of abusive or absent caregivers.

- Jesus said, "Be sons of your Father who is in heaven; for He causes His sun to rise on the evil and the good, and sends rain on the righteous and the unrighteous" (Matthew 5:45). The Lord cares about evil and unrighteous people because He loves everyone.

- "Do you think lightly of the riches of His kindness and tolerance and patience, not knowing that the kindness of God leads you to repentance?" (Romans 2:4). When we finally grasp God's kindness to us, it wins our hearts so that we'll place our trust in Him and change how we live.

> Our faith must be based on what God has revealed in the Scriptures about Himself.

Now that you understand how your concept of God determines your faith, you might need to reconsider what you believe about Him. Make sure it lines up with what has been revealed in the Scriptures. Your concept of God is an extremely important factor that determines what you believe about His ability and willingness to answer your prayers. We'll examine these two things in the next chapter.

4 | ABLE + WILLING = ANSWER

"Our God whom we serve is *able* to deliver
us from the furnace of blazing fire; and
He *will* deliver us." (Daniel 3:17)

A farmer owned two mules named Willing and Able. Willing was eager to work, but was scrawny and struggled to pull the plow. On the other hand, Able was a powerful mule but stubborn. Whenever the farmer tried to get Able to pull the plow, he refused to move. Willing was willing, but not able. Able was able, but not willing. And that's why the farmer never got any work done.

Answered prayer requires two things—the ability of God and the will of God. God is *able* to answer our prayers. But is He is *willing* to do it? It takes both God's hand and His heart to bring His answer to our prayers.

When the Jews were in exile in Babylon, King Nebuchadnezzar made a huge statue of gold and commanded everyone to worship the image. Three young men named Shadrach, Meshach, and Abednego refused to kneel down to it.

Nebuchadnezzar threatened to throw them into a fiery furnace unless they bowed. They answered him, "If it be so, our God whom we serve is *able* to deliver us from the furnace of blazing fire; and He *will* deliver us out of your hand, O king" (Daniel 3:17).

They believed two things about God—that He was both *able* and *willing* to deliver them. And He did. The king ordered them to be thrown into the furnace, but the Lord protected them from being burned inside. They came walking out of the furnace unharmed and their clothes didn't even smell like smoke (see Daniel 3:19–27). When God's power flows according to His will, prayers are answered and miracles take place.

ABLE + WILLING = ANSWER

I'm not saying this is a formula that automatically guarantees the answer to your prayers. Other factors may be involved, which will be discussed later. Able + Willing simply means we must be convinced of both before any answer becomes possible. Jesus told us to pray for God's will to be done on earth as it is in heaven. Obviously, His will isn't always done or He wouldn't tell us to pray for it to be done.

Some people doubt God's ability to answer their prayers. Others question whether or not He's willing to do it. Here are two examples of people in the Bible who made requests in prayer but only focused on half of the requirements.

It takes both God's hand and His heart
to bring His answer to our prayers.

EXAMPLE 1—BELIEVING GOD IS WILLING BUT NOT SURE HE IS ABLE

A father brought his demon-possessed son to Jesus. The man believed it was God's will for his son to be delivered but wasn't sure if Jesus was able to cure him. The father cried out, "If You can do anything, take pity on us and help us!" (Mark 9:22).

WILLING − ABLE = UNBELIEF

Jesus answered, "If You can! All things are possible to him who believes" (Mark 9:23). He challenged the father to think outside the box. Jesus, who never lied, promised that we will never encounter a problem that is too difficult for God to solve. "Behold, I am the LORD, the God of all flesh; is anything too difficult for Me?" (Jeremiah 32:27).

If we take Him at His word—and we can—the limitations of this natural world no longer hold us down. God can override natural laws to bring His answer to pass.

As Maxwell Smart would say, "I find that hard to believe."

Of course it's hard to believe, if you're always trying to figure out *how* God will bring your prayer to pass. You're still thinking inside the box. Don't focus on the difficulty of the problem but on God's supernatural ability.

What is God able to do? "[He] *is able* to do exceeding abundantly beyond all that we ask or think" (Ephesians 3:20). His power is unlimited, no matter what you're going through.

Do you think you've done so many bad things that the Lord won't help you? "*God is able* to make all grace abound to you" (2 Corinthians 9:8). His grace is greater than all your faults and will give you the ability to accomplish His will.

Are you exhausted, burned out, and lacking energy? "*God is able* to raise men even from the dead" (Hebrews 11:19). If He can bring people back from death, He can give you the strength you need to live through any difficulty.

Do you feel defeated by sin and trapped in bondage? "[He] *is able* to keep you from stumbling" (Jude 1:4). He will give you the power to live victoriously over sin.

Are you having a hard time believing that God will fulfill His promises to you? The Lord promised Abraham that he would have a son when he was nearly a hundred years old and his wife Sarah was ninety. Instead of doubting, Abraham was "fully assured that what He had promised, *He was able* also to perform" (Romans 4:21).

Are you beginning to grasp the power of our great Lord? Jesus revealed to us that nothing is impossible with God, and that the things impossible with men are possible with Him (Luke 1:37; 18:27).

Of course, just because all things are possible with God doesn't mean everything we request will come to pass. God's ability must work according to His will. Presumption is believing in the ability of God apart from the will of God, which can bring disastrous consequences.

ABILITY – WILL = PRESUMPTION

If Satan cannot get us to doubt God's power, he will try to get us to presume upon His will. In fact, the devil devised a plan to separate God's ability from His will when he tempted Jesus in the wilderness. He wanted the Son of God to believe in the Father's ability to perform miracles but to *ignore His will*.

Jesus was hungry after not eating anything for forty days. Satan tempted Him to turn some stones into bread instead of waiting for God's provision. His Father had spoken from heaven when He was baptized, saying, "This is my beloved Son, in whom I am well pleased" (Matthew 3:17). The devil taunted Him, "If you are the Son of God, command that these stones become bread" (Matthew 4:3).

Performing this miracle should have been no problem—if He really did have miraculous powers as the Son of God. Although Jesus would later turn water into wine, He knew that the wilderness wasn't the right place to perform His first miracle. Nor would He try to prove to the devil that He could do it. He had the ability to rearrange the molecules in the rocks so that they would become tasty bread, but it wasn't the Father's will. Water into wine, yes. Stones into bread, no.

When his first temptation failed, Satan tried again to get Jesus to presume upon His Father and force God to work against His will. The devil took Jesus to the pinnacle of the temple and challenged Him to jump off. If He was God's Son, His Father would surely protect Him. Satan even quoted Psalm 91:11–12 to remind Him that the angels would catch Him before He hit the ground.

Satan tempted Jesus *with Scripture*. What an unlikely tool to tempt someone with—the very words of God. No one would suspect that the Word of God, taken out of context, could be an instrument of temptation. This was one of those rare cases where Satan *wanted* the person he was tempting to trust God. Trust in His ability, but ignore His will.[3]

Jesus answered, "You shall not put the Lord your God to the test." To say it another way, you shall not try to force God to do something against His will. If Jesus had jumped off the pinnacle He would have obeyed Satan's orders instead of His Father, and the angels would not have caught Him.

EXAMPLE 2—BELIEVING GOD IS ABLE BUT NOT SURE HE IS WILLING

A leper came to Jesus and said, "If You are willing, You can make me clean" (Mark 1:40). The sick man believed in Jesus' ability to perform the miracle but wasn't sure He was willing.

Jesus was moved with compassion, touched him, and said, "I am willing; be cleansed" (Mark 1:41). God released His ability according to His will.

ABLE + WILLING = ANSWERED PRAYER

In another situation, the disciples were crossing the Sea of Galilee in the middle of the night when they encountered a storm. In their time of need, Jesus came walking to them on the water. Peter called out, "Lord, if it's you, tell me to come." He believed that God could give him the ability to walk on the water but wasn't sure if it was His will.

When Peter heard Jesus say "Come," he knew it was God's will for him to get out of the boat and walk on the water. Peter believed he could actually step on the waves, which was definitely thinking outside the box. But after walking a few steps toward Jesus, Peter heard the angry waves shouting, "You can't do that!" He listened to his logic and lost faith in God's ability to keep him on top of the water.

His faith scampered back inside the box, which caused him to sink. Even though he doubted, Jesus didn't let him drown. He lifted him up and they climbed back into the boat.

PRAYING IN GOD'S WILL

When it comes to prayer, we must first find the answer to these two important questions. *Is God able*? The Scriptures clearly reveal that nothing is too difficult for God. It's a matter of our believing that what God says about himself is true. *Is God willing*? The answer to this question isn't as clear as the first. Every situation is different and God is the only one who knows the answer to this question. He does tell us:

> This is the confidence which we have before Him, that, *if we ask anything according to His will*, He hears us. And if we know that He hears us in whatever we ask, we know that we have the requests which we have asked from Him. (1 John 5:14–15)

The secret of answered prayer is to believe in God's ability and to ask according to His will. How do we know if we are asking correctly? Sometimes knowing His will isn't so obvious. Here are three ways that we can pray outside of God's will.

We're praying out of God's will . . .

1. IF WE ASK WITH THE WRONG MOTIVES

Sometimes it takes a while to figure out that we've been asking for something the Lord doesn't want us to have. Often we want our own will to be done rather than His. God always knows the motives behind our prayers. James wrote, "You ask and don't receive *because you ask wrongly,* so that you may spend it on your desires for pleasure" (James 4:3 HCSB).

Let's clear up a common misunderstanding. Having a strong desire for something doesn't automatically make it selfish. Sometimes God puts a particular desire in our hearts while at other times it's just coming from us. Psalm 37:3 says, "Delight yourself in the LORD and He will give you the desires of your heart." When we submit ourselves to the Lord, He will place His desires in our hearts so that we will want what He desires for us. He'll make us able to see that His plans for us are best.

2. IF OUR REQUEST DISAGREES WITH GOD'S WORD

Second Timothy 2:13 says it is impossible for God to deny Himself, so He will not grant requests that contradict His Word.

Kenneth Bruner, the stepson of a minister, gathered his seven accomplices together for prayer before they robbed a store. Bruner asked God for His divine protection while they held up Herman's Fine Jewelry in Des Moines, Iowa.[4]

He conveniently ignored the eighth commandment, which says, "Thou shalt not steal" (Exodus 20:15). The Lord won't bless burglaries, reward robbers, or compensate crooks. However, God did send the police to escort Bruner & Company safely to jail.

Bruner asked the Lord to assist them but God sent the cops to arrest them.

I doubt you'll ever ask God's help for you to rob a store but you might ask Him for other things that contradict what He has revealed in the Bible. Make sure what you are praying for lines up with the Scriptures. The Lord only wants the very best for you.

3. IF OUR PRIORITIES ARE WRONG

Some things aren't wrong in themselves, but we've turned them into idols. Is the object of your affection greater than your love for God? The apostle John wrote to Christians, not pagans, when he said, "Little children, guard yourselves from idols" (1 John 5:21). An idol is anything or anyone that is more important to you than Him. When our priorities are out of order, the Lord will be more interested in getting *us* right than granting our requests.

A certain employee misused his business credit card. The company he worked for allowed him to use the card for business purchases only. Although he could use the credit card at his discretion, the company had set up certain parameters for its use. The man decided to misuse his privilege to purchase a number of items for himself. The company fired him when they discovered he was using it against their will.

Our Father in heaven has given us a "credit card" called prayer to fulfill His purposes on earth. One reason for prayer is to meet our needs. Although we can use the privilege at any time, He always wants to approve the way we use it.

Some Christians are deprived of the benefits because they *won't use* the privilege. Others are denied of the benefits because they *misuse* the privilege. But our willingness to pray and the Father's willingness to approve our request will always bring the answer we need.

What if you are praying for something that isn't mentioned in Scripture? How can you know with certainty that you're praying according to God's will? If you will seek Him with all your heart, He will reveal His plan to you. The Holy Spirit will bear witness with your spirit for the things He wants.

Trust His ability. Follow His will.

5 | NOT "HOW" BUT "WHO"

"Behold, I am the LORD, the God of all flesh;
is anything too difficult for Me?" (Jeremiah 32:27)

One of the greatest hindrances to faith is trying to figure out *how* God will answer your prayers. It's going to be hard for you to trust God if you are continually wondering how He will intervene in your circumstances to change your situation.

Quit asking yourself, "How is it possible? How can God do it? How does He perform miracles?" That's for God to handle. (He's probably not going to tell you anyway.)

When the blind man begged for Jesus to give him sight, he didn't ask Him to explain how He would do it: "Before you heal me, could you please clarify exactly how you are going to do this miracle? It's a problem with my optic nerve, isn't it? Since you don't have a scalpel to perform surgery, how are you going to get inside my head to make the needed repairs?"

Even if the blind man had asked, Jesus would not have answered, "Those are great questions that deserve an explanation. Here's exactly how I plan to do the miracle and restore your sight . . ."

Of course, Jesus never explained to anyone how He gave sight to the blind, hearing to the deaf, or life to the dead. Even if He had explained how He did it, do you really think anyone would have understood? Logic isn't capable of grasping the supernatural ways of God. The Lord spoke these words through Isaiah the prophet:

"My thoughts are not your thoughts, neither are your ways My ways," declares the Lord. "For as the heavens are higher than the earth, so are My ways higher than your ways, and My thoughts than your thoughts." (Isaiah 55:8–9)

God's thoughts and ways are beyond our understanding. Since He knows the outcome of every possible situation and the best timing to make things happen for us, we won't be able to figure out *how* or *when* He will answer our prayers. We must place these two mysteries in His hands and trust Him completely.

If my computer gets a glitch, I don't need to understand *how* to fix it. I just need to know a person *who* can repair computers. I don't need a technical explanation about what he or she is doing to resolve the issue. I simply need to trust in the expert's ability to correct the problem.

If I am a single person and praying for Him to bring my future spouse, I don't need to understand *how* I will find the right person. I just need to trust in the God *who* is able to bring us together. If I don't know what to do in a difficult situation, I must trust the Lord to give me wisdom and direction.

So instead of wondering "how," shift your focus to "who." Keep your eyes fixed on the supernatural God who is able to do what's humanly impossible. Fix your attention on the ability of God instead of the difficulty of your situation. "Trust in the LORD with all your heart and do not lean on your own understanding" (Proverbs 3:5).

Fix your attention on the ability of God instead of the difficulty of your situation.

WHEN ZACHARIAS ASKED "HOW," GABRIEL ANSWERED "WHO"

In Luke 1, we learn that Zacharias had prayed for a child. We don't know when he started praying for his wife Elizabeth to become pregnant, but it was probably when they were much younger. When nothing happened, he assumed his prayer had never been heard by God.

Years passed. Elizabeth was now elderly, far beyond her physical ability to become pregnant. Zacharias had deteriorated from a powerful young dude to a pitiful old dud. His prayer requests to become a father were still recorded on the yellowed pages of his prayer journal but dismissed long ago from his mind. It was just too late. Or was it?

One day while he was performing his temple duty, the angel Gabriel appeared to the right of the altar of incense. Zacharias was terrified. You would be scared too if a glowing spiritual being suddenly appeared in front of you. And what the angel told him was just as shocking. "Your petition has been heard, and your wife Elizabeth will bear you a son, and you will give him the name John" (Luke 1:11–13).

Zacharias wanted his prayer answered, but he might not have wanted it answered this late in the ball game. It almost sounds like a joke. God always has His reasons why He delays the answers to our prayers. He had an important task for Zacharias's son John, and He brought him into the world at just the right time to fulfill His purposes.

Gabriel went on to explain what John would accomplish in the future *after he became an adult* (Luke 1:15–17). This shows that the answer to Zacharias's prayer had far greater ramifications than he could have ever imagined. (And so do our prayers.) God had plans to use Zacharias's future son, John, to prepare people's hearts to receive the Messiah, who would die for the sins of the entire world.

If I were looking for a sign that my prayer had been answered, an angelic visitation would be a good one. Not many people have one of God's messengers make a personal appearance to announce that their prayers have been heard. Zacharias was staring at possibly the highest-ranking angel in heaven, Gabriel, "who stands in the presence of God" (Luke 1:19). The Lord informed Gabriel about Elizabeth's pregnancy and dispatched him to tell Zacharias the exciting news.

To grasp the significance of this announcement, remember that Zacharias and Elizabeth were both "advanced in years" (Luke 1:7) and could very well have been eighty years old at this time. The same Greek phrase "advanced in years" is used in Luke 2:37 of Anna, who was eighty-four.

Elizabeth and Zacharias were probably married around age twenty and started praying for a child. Ten years pass. "Lord, *please* answer our prayer." No answer. Another ten years go by. "God, have we done something wrong? Don't you love us?" Again, they hear no answer.

Elizabeth advances to the age when she is no longer able to have a child. They probably stopped praying when she hit menopause and assumed the answer was no. She turns sixty, then seventy, then eighty. They can't understand why God never answered them, yet they both continue to walk faithfully with the Lord. They never get angry at Him for apparently not answering their request.

Then one day Zacharias is chosen to serve in the temple. Because of the large number of priests in Israel, this would be the only time during his life he was allowed to enter the sanctuary and burn incense. The people who served in the temple were chosen by lot, and his name had never been drawn prior to this. The timing wasn't right, so God prevented it from happening.

So it was no accident that Zacharias's lot was chosen on this day, because after he entered the temple, the angel Gabriel appeared to him to the right of the altar. He *called Zacharias and Elizabeth by name* and informed them that their petition had been heard. Yes, the prayer they had prayed sixty years before was now answered!

Instead of rejoicing over this good news, Zacharias scratched his head in unbelief. He asked, "*How* shall I know this for certain? For I am an old man, and my wife is advanced in years" (Luke 1:18). Gabriel had told him *who* answered his prayer, but Zacharias wanted to know *how* this miracle would happen.

When it comes to prayer, make sure you don't listen to Mr. Logic's advice. Mr. Logic is that invisible little guy who sits on your shoulder and explains why something won't work. Gabriel's astounding announcement didn't compute in Zacharias's mind. He probably wanted to say, "Can you give me a little more proof, like writing the date of his birth in the sky? I'm thinking of a number between one and a thousand. What is it?"

Zacharias couldn't imagine how his elderly wife could conceive, so he asked how he would know for certain. The angelic visitation just wasn't enough confirmation for him. He wanted Gabriel to go into more detail so he could fully understand in medical terms exactly how the miracle would take place. He didn't realize he had just made *another* request—to be told how could he know with certainty that the angel's message was true. His inquiring mind wanted to know.

There's nothing wrong with an inquiring mind—unless your curiosity leads you to doubt God when He's actually answering your prayers! Since Zacharias refused to believe this announcement, Gabriel gave him a miraculous sign that would silence him from asking another question. He would be unable to talk for the next nine months. Like an episode out of *Bewitched,* Zacharias found himself mouthing words without making sounds. That's how he would know for certain.

When Mary asked "how," Gabriel answered "who"

Six months later, God sent Gabriel to announce another miraculous pregnancy. This time he wasn't appearing to an old man but to a young virgin chosen by the Lord. She lived in the little town of Nazareth, about sixty-five miles up the road from Jerusalem. And Gabriel knew exactly where to find her.

Again, he appeared suddenly and told Mary, "Hail, favored one! The Lord is with you. Do not be afraid, for you have found favor with God. You will conceive in your womb, and bear a son, and you shall name Him Jesus" (Luke 1:28–31). And just as he did with Zacharias, Gabriel went on to explain *what Jesus would do as an adult* and how He would impact eternity by reigning over a kingdom that will have no end (Luke 1:30–33).

Mary asked, "*How* can this be, since I am a virgin?" Just like Zacharias, she wanted to know how it would come to pass.

She asked *how,* but Gabriel answered *who.* "The Holy Spirit will come upon you, and the power of the Most High will overshadow you" (Luke 1:35). It was as if he had answered, "Mary, don't try to understand how, but trust the Holy Spirit who has the power to make it happen."

You're probably wondering why Gabriel didn't tell her, "Behold, you will be unable to speak until the day you give birth because you didn't believe me." That's how he dealt with Zacharias, so why not Mary too?

The reason was because she hadn't been praying to become pregnant the way Zacharias and Elizabeth had prayed. Mary had been selected and "favored" by God to give birth to His Son, even though she was a virgin. She deserved an explanation. Most importantly, though, when Mary heard Gabriel's explanation about *who* would bring this miracle about, she immediately believed him and said, "May it be done to me according to your word" (Luke 1:37). Zacharias wasn't satisfied with God's response to his own prayer, but Mary only had to hear that God was the one who would work the miracle in order to believe. When Mary went to Elizabeth to tell her the good news, the older woman greeted her by saying, "Blessed is she who believed that there would be a fulfillment of what had been spoken to her by the Lord!" (Luke 1:45).

Learning to Trust God

If you want your faith in God to increase, quit trying to figure out *how* your prayer request will come to pass. Instead, focus your attention on the Lord, *who* can do the impossible. Jesus assured us He can do anything. "With men it is impossible, but not with God; for all things are possible with God" (Mark 10:27).

I don't know how elderly Elizabeth became fertile, but I know who did it.

I don't know how Mary became pregnant as a virgin, but I know who did it.

I don't know how five thousand people were fed with five loaves, but I know who did it.

I don't know how a blind man's sight was restored, but I know who did it.

I don't know how the ten lepers were instantly healed, but I know who did it.

I don't know how Lazarus was raised from the dead, but I know who did it.

I don't know how it's possible to walk on water, but I know who did it.

I don't need to know *how* as long as I know *who*.

Place your trust in God "who is able to do exceedingly abundantly beyond all that we ask or think" (Ephesians 3:20).

Zacharias and Elizabeth had no idea that their prayer for a child as a young married couple started a chain reaction of events that would literally change the world. Their son, John the Baptist, became the greatest of the Old Testament prophets (Matthew 11:9–13). He preached to Israel about their need to repent and prepared them to receive the teaching of Jesus.

So if you've been praying for something and God seems silent, just remember the example of Zacharias and Elizabeth. Remove the deadline you've placed on God. Continue to live faithfully for the Lord, even when it looks like your prayer isn't being answered.

And quit asking "how."

PRAYER

Heavenly Father, thank you for hearing my prayers even when it seems to me like nothing is happening. I place my situation in your hands and trust you with the outcome. I will quit trying to figure out how you will answer my prayer. I will fix my faith completely on you and not keep concentrating on my problem. I love and trust you. In Jesus' name.

6 | THE NATURAL REALM VS. THE SPIRITUAL REALM

> "For the things which are seen are
> temporal, but the things which are not
> seen are eternal." (2 Corinthians 4:18)

An atheist told a Christian, "You've got it all wrong about this God stuff. He doesn't exist."

"Why do you say that?" the Christian asked.

"Well, one time I was ice fishing in the Arctic, far away from the nearest village, when a blizzard hit. I couldn't see a thing and knew I would never get out of there alive. So I got down on my knees and prayed, 'God, I know that I've always denied your existence, but now I'm not sure. If you're real . . . if you really do exist, please help me and get me out of here.'"

"Well, didn't He help you get out of there?"

"Heck no, God didn't lift a finger. Some Eskimo appeared out of nowhere and led me out."

Some people refuse to acknowledge God because they only believe what they can see. But there's more to our existence than what's visible to our eyes. Faith is the ability to look past the natural realm. We read in the book of Hebrews, "Now faith is the assurance of things hoped for, the conviction of things not seen" (11:1). This verse describes two different characteristics of faith.

First, *faith concerns things we want to happen.* "Now faith is the assurance of *things hoped for . . .*" Hope always expects good things to happen, which is an important ingredient of faith. Hope gives faith its energy. Worry is the opposite of faith and expects bad things to happen, which drains our energy. When we have faith in God's promises, not only do we believe that they're going to come true, we're also eagerly awaiting their fulfillment.

Second, *faith concerns things we can't see.* "Now faith is . . . the conviction of *things not seen.*" There are some things that we haven't seen because we weren't there. None of us were there when Jesus restored the blind man's sight or raised Lazarus from the dead, but we have faith that the miracles happened exactly as recorded in the Gospels. But there's also another category of "things not seen"—things that we couldn't possibly see because they're immaterial and invisible. Faith understands that an invisible world exists beyond the earthly realm. Paul writes, "By [the Son] all things were created, both in the heavens and on earth, *visible and invisible*" (Colossians 1:16). God himself is called "the invisible, only God" (1 Timothy 1:17).

Imagine a horizontal line that divides the things we can see from the things we can't see. Everything "below the line" is visible, exists in the earthly realm, and will pass away. This world we live in often seems like the only reality. But there's another realm of existence, too—"above the line." Everything "above the line" is invisible, exists in the spiritual realm, and will last forever. God Himself is "above the line," since, as Jesus taught, "God is spirit" (John 4:24). But God also came down into the visible realm in the person of Jesus Christ. When He became a human being in the visible realm and then ascended in His resurrected body to the Father, He opened the way for us to reach Him in the spiritual realm through prayer.

The Two Realms

"Things which are not seen"
Spiritual Realm (Above the line)

Natural Realm (Below the line)
"Things which are seen"

The following verses contrast these two realms:

> While we look not at the *things which are seen* [below the line], but at the *things which are not seen* [above the line]; for the things which are seen are temporal [below the line], but the things which are not seen are eternal [above the line]. (2 Corinthians 4:18)

> Therefore if you have been raised up with Christ, keep seeking the *things above* [above the line], where Christ is, seated at the right hand of God. Set your mind on the *things above* [above the line], not on the things that are on earth [below the line]. (Colossians 3:1–2)

The Bible tells us about invisible things that exist in the spiritual realm, such as God and angels, Satan and demons, heaven and hell, and "treasure in heaven." These invisible things seem like foolishness to those who only believe in what they see in the earthly realm. Paul writes, "But a natural man" (that is, someone who only believes in the world of "nature" that he can see) "does not accept the things of the Spirit of God, for they are foolishness to him and he cannot understand them, *because they are spiritually appraised*" (1 Corinthians 2:14).

Since we cannot see the invisible spiritual realm, how do we know the Bible is telling us the truth about it? The proof is found in the prophecies recorded in the Scriptures that have already been fulfilled. We're not talking about the end-of-the-world prophecies which are still in the future, but the predictions by the Old Testament prophets that have already come to pass in history exactly as they had prophesied.

The prophet Micah (5:2) predicted over seven hundred years into the future that the Messiah would be born in Bethlehem, which was fulfilled by Jesus. The prophet Zechariah (11:12–13) predicted the Messiah would be betrayed for thirty pieces of silver and the money would be thrown in the sanctuary. This was fulfilled when Judas accepted thirty pieces of silver to betray Jesus and later threw down the coins in the temple (Matthew 26:15; 27:3–10). The Old Testament records hundreds of prophecies that were fulfilled exactly as predicted.[5]

Since the Bible can accurately predict the future, it proves itself to be true. This means we can trust God's Word about everything it reveals concerning the invisible spiritual realm, including the promises He has made to us that are recorded in the Scriptures.

PRAYER REACHES INTO THE SPIRITUAL REALM

Whenever we pray, we reach into the spiritual realm through Jesus' name and ask God to intervene in our situations here on earth. A Roman centurion had a need in the natural realm so he went to Jesus requesting healing for his servant. Jesus said, "I will come and heal him." The centurion humbly replied:

> "Lord, I am not worthy for you to come under my roof, but *just say the word* and my servant will be healed. For I, too, am a man under authority, with soldiers under me; and I say to this one, 'Go!' and he goes, and to another, 'Come!' and he comes and to my slave, 'Do this!' and he does it." (Matthew 8:8–9)

This centurion, who was in charge of a hundred soldiers, was referring to the military chain of command. When he said, "I, *too,* am a man under authority," he understood that Jesus received His authority by submitting to His Father in heaven. This centurion received his authority by submitting to the emperor on earth.

He didn't have to force the soldiers to obey. He could simply tell them what to do and they would immediately obey because his word carried authority. When the centurion said "Go" it was the same as if the emperor had said it. He knew Jesus could tell the slave's infirmity to leave and it would have to obey, just like the centurion could command a soldier to leave. When Jesus said "Your slave is healed," He was speaking on earth with all of the authority of God in heaven.

> When Jesus heard this He marveled and said to those who were following, "Truly I say to you, I have not found such great faith with anyone in Israel." (Matthew 8:10)

The Greek word "marveled" means to be astonished or astounded. The Gospels record that Jesus was astonished twice. First, He was astonished at the *unbelief* and hardness of heart of the people at Nazareth (Mark 6:6).[6] Second, He was astonished at the *great faith* of the centurion. This Roman soldier grasped an incredible spiritual truth, even though he hadn't been taught the Scriptures in a Jewish synagogue.

This Gentile had greater faith than anyone in Israel. Why? Because he understood that faith is established by submitting and yielding completely to God. He realized that genuine faith can reach into the spiritual realm and bring things to pass in the earthly realm. His faith was based on knowing that Jesus had received spiritual authority from His Father to work miracles in the natural world. The centurion didn't have to watch Jesus touch his servant. He knew if Jesus would simply speak the word (which he couldn't see), the miracle would occur. When the centurion returned home, he found his servant completely healed.

Today, all Jesus has to do is speak the word from heaven and it will be done, which is how God did miracles in the Old Testament. "[The people of Israel] cried out to the LORD in their trouble. He saved them out of their distresses. *He sent His word* and healed them, and delivered them from their destructions" (Psalm 107:19–20).

JESUS CAN OVERRULE THE EARTHLY REALM

On another occasion, Jesus was in a boat with His disciples on the Sea of Galilee when a terrible storm arose. Huge waves were breaking over the side and the boat was filling up with water. Jesus was soundly sleeping in the stern when the frightened disciples cried out for Him to save them. He got up and rebuked the wind and said to the sea, "Hush, be still!"

Immediately the wind stopped blowing and the sea became perfectly calm. The disciples said, "Who then is this, that even the wind and the sea obey Him?" (Mark 4:37–41). Here again we see that Jesus simply spoke the command, and the wind and sea in the natural realm obeyed Him. He also demonstrated His authority to overrule the natural realm when He said to the fig tree, "No longer shall there ever be any fruit from you"—at which the tree promptly withered in obedience (Matthew 21:19).

Jesus taught that it's possible to speak by faith to a mountain and cast it into the sea (Matthew 21:21; Mark 11:23). Why would anyone talk to a mountain? Mountains, wind, sea, and fig trees don't have ears, so these examples reveal to us that speaking words can serve a purpose outside of communicating with people. The words we speak are manifestations of what we believe in our hearts. Jesus said, "For the mouth speaks out of that which fills the heart" (Matthew 12:34). Romans 10:8 says, " 'The word is near you, in your mouth and in your heart'—that is, the word of faith which we are preaching."

Faith is trusting in God's ability to bring His will to pass in the natural realm. He can change our circumstances when we submit completely and call out to Him in prayer. True faith in God understands that He can do anything and that He has the last word in everything.

Faith Is the Ability to See Past the Physical Realm into the Spiritual Realm

Once you grasp the fact that there are two realms, natural and spiritual, you'll find that they're mentioned throughout the Bible. Here are some verses from the New Testament that describe the differences between the two realms. May these verses encourage you to pray to the living God in the spiritual realm.

Jesus said, "The things that are impossible with people [natural realm] are possible with God [spiritual realm]." (Luke 18:27)

Jesus said, "If I told you earthly things [natural realm] and you do not believe, how will you believe if I tell you heavenly things [spiritual realm]?" (John 3:12)

By faith we understand that the worlds [natural realm] were prepared by the word of God, so that what is seen [natural realm] was not made out of things which are visible [spiritual realm]. (Hebrews 11:3)

[Abraham] was looking for the city which has foundations [spiritual realm], whose architect and builder is God. (Hebrews 11:10)

By faith Moses . . . left Egypt, not fearing the wrath of the king [natural realm]; for he endured, as seeing Him who is unseen [spiritual realm]. (Hebrews 11:27)

We cannot see what is going on in the spiritual realm when we pray, so this is where our faith in God comes in. As we saw in this chapter, faith is conviction or evidence about the *things not seen*. The next chapter explores the importance of trusting in the Lord's ability and power when we pray.

7 | THE OBJECT OF YOUR FAITH

> "When the Son of Man comes, will He
> find faith on the earth?" (Luke 18:8)

We have zero chance of pleasing God if we don't have faith in Him—it's impossible. "Without faith it is impossible to please Him, for he who comes to God must believe that He is, and that He is a rewarder of those who diligently seek Him" (Hebrews 11:6).

The Lord loves to see His people taking steps of faith by trusting Him. "For we walk by faith, not by sight" (2 Corinthians 5:7). As we travel through this earthly life, we don't just take into account things we can see, but we also realize the reality of things we can't see in the spiritual realm. Hebrews 11:6 states two things we must believe, or two essential components of faith.

First, we must believe that *God exists.* He isn't a figment of our imagination. We must understand that a supernatural Being created all things and that after we die everyone will stand before Him.

Second, we must believe that *God rewards* those who diligently seek Him. Imagine what God would be like if He had made the entire world but never wanted us to search for Him or have a relationship with Him. That's not the kind of God we would want to have faith in! True faith seeks to know the true God, the one who loves us, rewards us, and wants us to be with Him forever. When we make Him our highest priority, He promises to bless us both in this world and in the life to come. Jesus said, "Pray to your Father who is in secret, and your Father who sees what is done in secret will reward you" (Matthew 6:6). Answering our prayers is one of the ways He rewards us in this world. "Whatever we ask we receive from Him, because we keep His commandments and do the things that are pleasing in His sight" (1 John 3:22).

As mentioned in the previous chapter, faith involves things we'd like to happen and things we can't see in the natural realm. "Faith is the assurance of things hoped for, the conviction of things not seen" (Hebrews 11:1).

After His resurrection Jesus said, "Blessed are they that have *not seen*, and yet believed" (John 20:29). Even though we weren't present to witness the resurrected Christ, we know in our hearts that He did rise from the dead. The Bible teaches us that this faith is all-important: "If you confess with your mouth Jesus as Lord, and believe in your heart that God raised Him from the dead, you will be saved" (Romans 10:9). This faith also shapes the way we should pray.

CHARACTERISTICS OF FAITH

1. FAITH TRUSTS IN THE PROMISES OF GOD.

Faith refuses to panic and is confident that God will come through. "So then faith comes by hearing, and hearing by the word of God" (Romans 10:17 NKJV). Yes, it does matter who you're listening to! Faith means we trust what God has promised in His Word, in spite of the way things may appear at the moment. "For every one of God's promises is 'Yes' in Him" (2 Corinthians 1:20 HCSB).

All throughout the Bible we find people who chose to believe what God had promised, even when their circumstances told them otherwise. Sarah was the first woman in history to go through menopause before she got pregnant. Zacharias' wife, Elizabeth, was the second. Sarah looked past the natural realm and saw that all things are possible with God. "By faith even Sarah herself received ability to conceive, even beyond the proper time of life, since *she considered Him faithful who had promised*" (Hebrews 11:11).

It is not enough just to know about God's promises. We must apply the Scriptures to our own situation to make them a reality. When prospectors discovered gold during the California Gold Rush in the 1800s, they had to "stake a claim." Staking a claim meant that they had to drive posts into the ground to claim the marked property as their own.

Although you cannot see God, you can see His promises recorded in the Bible. He wants you to stake a claim on them, which means receiving them as your own personal property. The fulfillment of each promise is God's responsibility. He fulfilled every promise He made to Israel and He will do the same for you. "Not one of the good promises which the LORD had made to the house of Israel failed; all came to pass" (Joshua 21:45).

> Although you cannot see God, you can see His promises recorded in the Bible.

2. FAITH BELIEVES THAT GOD HEARS OUR PRAYERS.

You've probably seen the old television commercial where the person is trying to get a cell phone signal and keeps repeating, "Can you hear me now? Hello . . . can you hear me now?" Sometimes we wonder if we're connecting with God when we talk to Him. "Can you hear me, Lord?"

When we pray we need to believe that the Lord hears us. If we don't believe He is listening, why would we even want to pray? "This is the confidence which we have before Him, that, if we ask anything according to His will, He hears us. And *if we know that He hears us* in whatever we ask, we know that we have the requests which we have asked from Him" (1 John 5:14–15). David said, "For the LORD has heard the voice of my weeping. The LORD has heard my supplication. The LORD receives my prayer" (Psalm 6:8–9).

3. Faith expects God to answer.

When Jesus passed through Jericho, a blind man named Bartimaeus cried out for mercy. "Jesus stopped and said, 'Call him here.' . . . And casting aside his cloak, he jumped up and came to Jesus" (Mark 10:49–50). Why does the Scripture point out that he threw his coat aside? I believe he was expecting to be healed and throwing his cloak aside was an act of faith. After he received his healing, he would be able to see where it was and pick it up.

At another time Jesus was teaching in Capernaum and many people had come to see Him. Four men brought a paralyzed man on a stretcher, hoping that Jesus would heal him. So many people had surrounded the house they couldn't get near the door.

What would you have concluded about the will of God in this situation? The circumstances made it appear as though the four men had wasted their time. When they saw the crowd around the house, they could have said, "I guess it's not God's will to heal our friend. The path to the front door would have been clear if He were going to heal him. We might as well go home."

Just because an obstacle is in your path doesn't mean what you desire is not God's will. Faith will find a way where there seems to be no way. These friends figured out how to get inside the house. They climbed on the roof, tore through the ceiling and lowered the paralyzed man on his stretcher in front of Jesus.

Imagine the people inside the house listening to Jesus teach when they hear a noise on the roof. They look up and see rays of sunshine shooting through an opening in the ceiling. Then Jesus stops teaching as the pallet with a paralyzed man comes to rest on the floor.

Jesus didn't say, "Who do you think you are, interrupting my sermon? And what are you doing, tearing up someone else's property? You're going to pay for this!"

He wasn't bothered by the damage to the roof or the interruption of His message. The Scripture tells us, "And *seeing their faith*, He said, 'Friend, your sins are forgiven you'" (Luke 5:20). While others saw the hole in the roof, Jesus saw their faith in Him.

This lame man in front of Him was far more important than the damaged roof above Him. Jesus then said something no one was expecting: "Your sins are forgiven." These four men didn't bring their friend to Jesus for his sins to be forgiven, but for his body to be healed.

But Jesus looks into the spiritual realm and can see things that we can't. No other person in the room saw the sins on this man's soul or the guilt he was carrying. Jesus examined the man's spiritual condition and saw he desperately needed forgiveness, which was a more serious matter than his infirmity. Physical healing is for this temporary world, but forgiveness of sins will last throughout eternity.

Was it God's will for the man to be healed? Even though his circumstances appeared to say no, Jesus said yes. He did heal him—and He did it in response to seeing the faith of his friends.

The Object of Your Faith

All faith, whether it's real or counterfeit, focuses on an object. It's easy to get caught up in what faith is supposed to be like—persevering, trusting, and so on—without actually asking *who* we should have faith in. Jesus told His disciples, "Have faith *in God*" (Mark 11:22). He told us to place our faith in the all-powerful, all-knowing God. This implies that it's possible for us to put our faith in a person or thing other than Him. If we place our trust in the wrong objects, when those things fall apart our faith will also fail. Jesus told Peter, "I have prayed for you, that your *faith may not fail*" (Luke 22:32).

Suppose you have strong faith that a frozen lake will hold you up if you walk on it. To prove your faith, you run and jump on the ice. Immediately you go crashing through into the frigid waters.

As you climb out, you say, "I just don't understand. I really believed the ice would hold me up. I had faith it would." Your faith failed because the object of your faith failed. You had faith in a weak object that was only a half-inch thick.

Some people have strong faith in weak objects. It's not enough to have strong faith. We must place our faith in an object that won't fail.

Now let's assume you have weak faith. You aren't sure the ice will hold you up, so you slowly edge out onto it. You're surprised to find the ice supports your weight. This time your faith didn't fail because the ice was ten inches thick. It wasn't your faith that held you up, but the thick ice. You simply placed your faith in a strong object that wouldn't fail.

I'd rather have weak faith on thick ice than strong faith on thin ice. Jesus Christ's death and resurrection is thick ice—the most important thing to believe. The apostle Paul wrote, "I delivered to you of *first importance* what I also received, that Christ died for our sins according to the Scriptures, and that He was buried, and that He was raised on the third day according to the Scriptures" (1 Corinthians 15:3–4).

Faith that won't fail is established on the historical fact that Jesus Christ rose from the dead and is alive today. The resurrection of Jesus is the foundation of our faith because if He had not overcome death, He would not be able to answer our prayers today. He is now in heaven and always lives to make intercession for us (Hebrews 7:25).

David wrote: "The LORD also will be a stronghold for the oppressed, a stronghold in times of trouble, and those who know Your name *will put their trust in You*. For You, O LORD, have not forsaken those who seek You" (Psalm 9:9–10). To "put" means to transfer something from one place to another. You withdraw money from your bank account and put it in your purse. When you refuel your vehicle, you transfer gas from the pump and put it in the tank of your car. So when you *put* your trust in the Lord, you transfer your confidence from yourself, or anything else, and place it in Him.

Wrong Objects of Faith

It's possible to put our faith in someone or something other than God. Here are three wrong objects in which we might be tempted to place our trust.

WRONG OBJECT 1—FAITH IN FAITH (SELF-CENTERED FAITH)

We can mistakenly put faith in *our own level of faith* instead of God. Having "faith in faith" turns our spiritual eyes inward rather than upward. This counterfeit faith makes us self-centered rather than God-centered as we try to conjure up faith from within instead of looking to Jesus.

At the end of an evangelistic meeting, a man approached a counselor asking about how to become a Christian. The counselor said, "You've got to *believe.* You've got to *believe* in Jesus. Do you believe?"

The man replied, "I'm trying to believe, but it's so hard." After trying for thirty minutes to muster up enough faith to believe in Jesus, he left the meeting frustrated.

The next night he returned to the church and talked with a different counselor. This time he trusted Jesus and became a Christian. Later he met the first counselor, who asked what had convinced him to have faith.

"He told me to believe in Jesus."

The first counselor said, "But that's what I told you to do last night."

"No, you told me I needed to *believe* in Jesus. He said I needed to believe in *Jesus.* You put the emphasis on having enough faith, but he put the emphasis on Christ and how He died for me. Once I focused on Him rather than myself, it was easy to believe."

Faith grows when it is placed in a great God who can do all things.

WRONG OBJECT 2— FAITH IN SOMEONE ELSE'S FAITH (SECOND-HAND FAITH)

It's easy to place our faith in someone who has faith, such as a godly mother or a pastor. But faith in someone else's faith is a second-hand faith. This kind of faith will also fail when it is tested, because it isn't genuine faith in Jesus.

Several Jewish exorcists attempted to cast out demons by saying, "I adjure you by Jesus *whom Paul preaches*" (Acts 19:13). The demon-possessed man beat them up, chasing them out of the house naked and wounded. They had not placed their faith in Jesus, but in Paul's faith in Jesus.

Some people even start questioning the existence of God because they put their faith in someone who doesn't believe in God, like a skeptical scientist or an atheist. They say, "This person is highly intelligent, so I will trust him and what he believes because it must be true." An atheist isn't someone who doesn't believe in God, but someone who *believes* there is no God. The Scripture explains why people choose to believe that God doesn't exist. Their atheistic faith is based "in the futility of their mind, being darkened in their understanding, excluded from the life of God because of the ignorance that is in them, because of the hardness of their heart" (Ephesians 4:18).

As the previous chapter explained, those who believe only in the earthly realm cannot comprehend the spiritual realm. "A natural man does not accept the things of the Spirit of God, for they are foolishness to him; and *he cannot understand them, because they are spiritually appraised*" (1 Corinthians 2:14).

The apostle Paul instructed us not to let those who don't believe in God to sway us. He said, "What then, if some did not believe, their unbelief will not nullify the faithfulness of God, will it?" (Romans 3:3). Don't let someone else's scoffing and unbelief influence your faith in the true God, even if they're arrogant and appear confident. "The wicked plots against the righteous and gnashes at him with his teeth. The LORD laughs at him, for He sees his day is coming" (Psalm 37:12–13).

Genuine faith comes directly from the Lord. Jesus asked His disciples, "Who do you say that I am?" Peter answered, "You are the Christ, the Son of the living God." Jesus answered, "Blessed are you Simon Barjona, because flesh and blood did not reveal this to you, but My Father who is in heaven" (Matthew 16:15–16).

Peter had first-hand faith, straight from the Father. That is the only kind of faith that is pleasing to God. Who do you believe Jesus is? I hope you won't answer, "Well, Peter said . . ." Don't put your faith in Peter's faith. Let the Father reveal His identity to you.

Wrong Object 3—Faith in things (Idolatry)

Some people place their faith in the government to meet their needs. Others put their faith in military strength to give them peace of mind. "Some boast in chariots, and some in horses, but we will boast in the name of the LORD, our God" (Psalm 20:7). Still others trust in their jobs, the strength of the economy, or their investments. All these things will ultimately fail.

Jesus said, "Make friends for yourselves by means of the unrighteous money so that *when it fails,* they may welcome you into eternal dwellings" (Luke 16:9 HCSB). He instructs us to use our money for eternal purposes. If we do that, it won't become an object that will fail but a tool to be used. Everything in the earthly realm will one day be destroyed. "And the world is passing away, and also its lusts; but the one who does the will of God abides forever" (1 John 2:17).

Place your faith in God alone and trust His Word to guide you. It will make a difference both now and in eternity.

8 | UNCLOGGING THE PIPELINE

"If I regard wickedness in my heart,
The Lord will not hear" (Psalm 66:18).

Not long after my wife and I bought our first house, something went wrong with our plumbing. We filled our kitchen sink with water to wash dishes, but when we pulled the drain plug out, the water level stayed the same. We called a plumber, who told us that too much food had gone down the drain at one time and had clogged up the pipe. He pulled out a plumber's tool and cleaned out the blockage, which opened the pipe and drained the water.

If it seems like your prayers aren't getting through, it might be because your pipeline to God is stopped up. We can actually sabotage our own prayers by allowing destructive attitudes to take root in our hearts. I'm not saying we have to be perfect before God hears us, but the Scriptures teach us that certain sins can block the answers to our prayers.

We can't intentionally clog up our hearts and think we can still expect God to answer our prayers as if everything is just fine. The Lord isn't going to grant every request and He designed prayer to shut down when we misuse the privilege. Listed below are five blockages that can hinder your prayers from being answered.

BLOCKAGE 1—UNBELIEF

Unbelief is a blockage that will keep prayers from being answered. Although Jesus wanted to heal many people in His hometown, "He did not do many miracles there because of their unbelief" (Matthew 13:58). It wasn't His unwillingness that halted the miracles, but *their* unwillingness to believe in Him. Just as we saw before, "he who comes to God must believe that He is"—that is, that He exists in the first place—"and that He is a rewarder of those who diligently seek Him" (Hebrews 11:6).

Tom was an acquaintance whom I had met through one of my friends. He worked as a janitor in a nearby church and as a security guard at our local hospital. When Tom walked it was as if he were stepping on thorns. One day I asked him if he had injured his feet.

"No, I was born with a problem with the nerves in my feet," he explained. "Doctors told me that surgery could not correct the problem and I would have to learn to live with it. I've had constant pain in my feet every day of my life. That's why I walk the way I do."

"Are you saying that you've never had a day in your life when your feet weren't hurting?"

"Not a single day."

"Can I pray for God to heal your feet?" I asked.

"Yeah, I guess so," he replied, as if he knew it wouldn't do any good.

"Lord," I prayed, "I ask you to have mercy on this man. The doctors say surgery can't help him but I know all things are possible with you. I ask you to heal his feet and take away the pain."

I didn't feel like anything had happened when I prayed. He didn't tell me that his feet tingled as I said the prayer, which would have been a nice confirmation of being healed. When I had finished praying, he slowly hobbled away, just like he had walked before.

Two days later I saw him walking down the street and I could hardly believe my eyes. He wasn't limping! I ran over to him, "Tom, you're walking normally. What happened?"

"Well, the day after you prayed I woke up and the pain was gone. I haven't had pain since then."

"That's amazing!" I exclaimed. "God did a miracle and healed your feet!"

I was stunned that he wasn't excited at all. He wasn't even smiling. He said, "The pain is gone *but I don't believe it.*"

"What? You don't believe it? How can you *not* believe it? The pain that you've had every day is gone!"

"I just don't believe it. It's just too hard to believe. The doctors said I would always have pain in my feet." As he walked away, I was dumbfounded.

A week later I saw him hobbling as he had before. When he saw me, he said, "Well, the pain came back, just like I thought it would. I knew it was too good to be true."

Why did he lose his healing? I believe God miraculously healed him in response to my prayer, but his unbelief prevented his healing from being permanent. He refused to acknowledge the miracle or thank God for healing Him. His reaction reminded me of the Scripture: "For even though they knew God, *they did not honor Him as God, or give thanks*, but they became futile in their speculations and their foolish heart was darkened" (Romans 1:21).

Unbelief refuses to acknowledge that God intervenes in our situations. Jesus did not do many miracles in His hometown due to the people's unbelief, and Tom's unbelief clogged the pipeline and stopped the complete healing in his feet from taking place. If he had given thanks to God for the miracle, I believe his feet would have remained healed.

God wants you to live with expectant faith, and He wants to hear you sincerely thank Him from your heart when He does answer your prayer.

BLOCKAGE 2—UNFORGIVENESS

One sign of unforgiveness is when you're continually angry at someone. Jesus explained that unforgiveness can clog your pipeline to heaven when He said, "Whenever you stand praying, if you have anything against anyone, forgive him" (Mark 11:25 NKJV).

You might think that what that person did to you is too big a debt to forgive. Nearly everyone uses that as an excuse. If your act of forgiveness is based on whether they deserve it, you'll never forgive anyone. You'll find the grace to forgive when you focus on what Jesus did for you on the cross—and not on what an evil person did to you. Whatever they did to you is insignificant compared to the enormous debt God has forgiven you.

> You'll find the grace to forgive when you focus on what Jesus did for you on the cross—and not on what an evil person did to you.

I cannot give away something unless I've first received it. I can't give you twenty dollars unless I've first received twenty dollars. I also can't offer forgiveness to someone unless I've first accepted forgiveness from God for my sins. If I've received fifty million dollars' worth of forgiveness from God, then I will be so grateful for what He did for me that I can easily give my enemy twenty dollars' worth of forgiveness. The key to forgiving others is to remember the incredible mercy God had on you. "For judgment will be merciless to one who has shown no mercy; mercy triumphs over judgment" (James 2:13).

It is impossible to forgive if you still feel hatred for your enemy, so you must change the way you view the person who hurt you. Forgiveness means releasing the anger out of your heart so you are not tormented anymore by what your enemy did to you.

Jesus told a parable about a slave who owed the king ten thousand talents that he couldn't repay. The king forgave and released him from the debt because he "felt compassion" for the slave (Matthew 18:27). Forgiveness flows out of compassion, which means to have pity on someone. When you forgive everyone who has hurt you and let go of the hurt, it unclogs the blockage that's keeping your prayers from being answered.

Blockage 3—Pride

Alexander Solzhenitsyn once said that pride grows in the human heart like lard on a pig. The Scripture says, "Clothe yourselves with humility toward one another, because God resists the proud but gives grace to the humble" (1 Peter 5:5 HCSB).

How would you like for God to resist everything you do? The Lord detests the sin of pride. A magnet can attract or repel depending on the direction it's facing. We can either attract God or repel Him, according to whether our hearts are facing toward Him or away from Him. He's attracted to those whose hearts are humble and sincere, but repels those who are self-sufficient and don't think they need Him.

When God sent Jonah to tell the evil people of Nineveh that their city would soon be destroyed, the citizens believed his message and repented. Even the king of Nineveh knew he needed to turn his life around:

> When the word reached the king of Nineveh, *he arose from his throne, laid aside his robe from him*, covered himself with sackcloth and sat on the ashes. He issued a proclamation and it said, "... Let men call on God earnestly that each may turn from his wicked way and from the violence which is in his hands. Who knows, God may turn and relent and withdraw His burning anger so that we will not perish."
>
> When God saw their deeds, that they turned from their wicked way, then God relented concerning the calamity which He had declared He would bring upon them. And He did not do it. (Jonah 3:6–10)

Humility requires you to step down from your throne and lay aside your robe of pride. When the king got off his throne and the citizens repented, it unclogged the pipeline and their prayers were answered by God. The Lord cancelled His coming judgment against Nineveh because they humbled themselves and stopped their evil behavior.

Humility requires you to step
down from your throne and lay
aside your robe of pride.

Most people think that pride means being arrogant, but arrogance is only one manifestation of pride. Pride is trusting in your own strength and abilities instead of depending on God.

Jesus told a parable about the Pharisees, whose hearts were clogged with pride. A Pharisee and a tax gatherer went into the temple to pray. Pharisees believed they were the closest people to God, while tax-collectors were considered the worst kind of sinners. The common people were convinced that the Pharisees had a hotline to God when they prayed, but Jesus challenged that idea by teaching a lesson about pride and humility.

> The Pharisee stood and was praying this *to himself*: "God, I thank You that I am not like other people: swindlers, unjust, adulterers, or even like this tax collector." . . . But the tax collector, standing some distance away, was even unwilling to lift up his eyes to heaven, but was beating his breast, saying, "God, be merciful to me, the sinner!" (Luke 18:11, 13)

The Pharisee thought he was praying to God, but he was actually praying to himself. Jesus ends the parable by declaring that the tax collector, who knew he was unworthy, was the one justified by God, and the Pharisee, who looked down on others, was the one who was condemned. Pride clogs the pipeline to God but humility opens the way to Him.

BLOCKAGE 4—WRONG MOTIVES

In the old comedy *The Man with Two Brains,* Steve Martin plays a brain surgeon whose wife has recently died. He quickly falls in love with a devious woman, Dolores, who is only after his money. Martin stands in front of a portrait of his deceased wife and asks, "If there is anything wrong with my feelings for Dolores, just give me a sign. Any sign at all."

Immediately the picture starts spinning around, the room starts to shake, lights flash on and off, and a voice screams, "No! . . . No! . . . No! . . . Noooooo!"

After everything settles back to normal, he says, "Just any kind of sign. I'll keep on the lookout for it."

In the next scene, he is standing at the altar with Dolores saying, "I do."

Of course, Dolores turns out to be his worst nightmare. Some people are determined to get what they want and won't change their mind no matter how many warnings and red flags are waved in their faces. Without even considering God's will, they'll pray and ask for His stamp of approval on what they've already decided to do.[7]

When God screams, "No! . . . No! . . . No! . . . Noooooo!" these people never hear Him. They might get what they want, but it's not because the Lord answered their prayer. Just because a person acquires something they lust for doesn't mean God gave it to them.

The Lord won't answer selfish requests that are prayed with the wrong motives. The apostle James explains, "You ask and don't receive because you ask with wrong motives, so that you may spend it on your evil desires" (James 4:3 HCSB). The Lord is too wise and caring to be manipulated by anyone.

An X-ray machine can look at a person's heart but it can't see the motives inside. But God is able to see inside our hearts and the intention behind every request. "All the ways of a man are clean in his own sight, but the LORD weighs the motives" (Proverbs 16:2).

People do things for a reason, even if it's the wrong reason. When detectives are trying to solve a murder case, the first question they ask is, "Who had a motive for doing this? Who would have benefited from this person's death?" The evil deed that took a person's life can be traced back to an evil motive in someone's heart.

We can pray for the wrong reasons. We pray "my will be done" instead of "Thy will be done." You might be head over heels in love with the wrong person, totally unaware of how that person may break your heart down the road. The Lord will do everything He can to stop you from making a huge mistake, but you still have a free will that He won't override.

God wants you to always ask with the right motives so that you won't misuse the answer He sends you. Once your motive lines up with His will, then your pipeline will get unclogged and He will answer your prayer in His right way and timing.

Blockage 5—Mistreating Others

Just as we can block the pipeline with unforgiveness, we can also close ourselves off from God by mistreating the people around us. The Scripture especially warns those who mistreat the people who are closest to them. "You husbands in the same way, live with your wives in an understanding way . . . show her honor as a fellow heir of the grace of life, *so that your prayers will not be hindered*" (1 Peter 3:7). This verse states that if a husband mistreats his wife, his threatening words and actions toward his spouse will keep his prayers from being answered.

The Lord sees what is happening behind closed doors, even if no one else knows. He's the one who answers prayers and will withhold His blessing until the spouses honor one another as the He says. "Husbands, love your wives, just as Christ also loved the church and gave Himself up for her" (Ephesians 5:25).

Obviously marriage consists of two people who interact. If a husband is not "living with his wife in an understanding way," the wife may be able to make a change in behavior happen more quickly by showing kindness toward her husband and praying for his heart to become sensitive to the Holy Spirit, who is the only one who can convert him.

The way you treat others reveals the authenticity of your relationship with God. "The one who does not love his brother whom he has seen, cannot love God whom he has not seen" (1 John 4:20). The answers to your prayers begin with treating others with kindness and grace.

PRAYER

Lord, forgive me for my unbelief. I will trust you even when I don't understand your ways. I forgive (*name the person*) for (*describe the offense*). I admit that I have been self-sufficient and have trusted in my own abilities rather than you. I humble myself before you. I desire that the motives in my heart will line up with your perfect will. I realize that I have not treated (*name the person*) in the right way and I will change the way I speak and act. I will unclog all the blockages that have hindered my prayers and thank you for hearing my prayer. And now I will patiently wait for your answer to my prayer with expectant faith in you!

9 | WHEN WILL THE ANSWER COME?

> "How long, O Lord? Will You forget me forever?
> How long will You hide Your face from me?"
> (Psalm 13:1)

A number of years ago my friend Max Wilkins, who is now president of The Mission Society, had stopped at a traffic light and was waiting for it to change. An elderly woman with a walker started hobbling across the street in front of his car just as the light turned green. The driver behind Max couldn't understand why he wouldn't go through the green light, so he started honking his horn.

As Max continued to wait for her, the man behind him stuck his head out the window and started yelling. Max got out of his car and walked back to the angry driver. He held out his keys and said, "If you want to run over her, then go ahead!"

By this time the hothead could clearly see the elderly lady inching her way across the street. He finally realized what had kept Max from moving forward. Max could see something that the other driver couldn't.

When we've prayed and are waiting for the answer to come, we can't understand why God isn't moving forward. From our perspective we see a green light. So we start honking our horn at God, never realizing He can see things that we can't.

God knows details about our situation that we don't. He sees the outcome down the road of every choice we make. Just because we don't see God doing something right now doesn't mean He's not at work. The Lord will often delay answers to our prayers for reasons we don't fully understand at the moment. It's during these times that we must trust the all-wise God who knows what He's doing—even when it might not make sense to us. Trusting Him will give us peace of mind.

Two common questions we ask when we pray are *how* and *when*. First, we ask, "*How* will you do the miracle that I need?" God isn't going to tell us.

Then we ask, "*When* will the answer come? How long will I have to wait?" Again, God isn't going to tell us. We may have prayed for something or someone for years, and nothing seems to be happening, so we wonder if we should stop praying. Is this doing any good? Is God even listening? Am I praying for something that's not in God's will? How long should I keep waiting before I quit praying?

In our fast-paced, instant gratification society we've lost the desire to wait for God's best. David prayed, "How long, O LORD? Will You forget me forever?" Even God's favored king had waited so long that he wondered if the Lord had forgotten about him. So don't lose hope when you are praying. Remember that God's delays are not His denials.

God's delays are not His denials.

GOD'S TIMING

God clearly has a timetable for events. The Father sent His Son into the world at precisely the right time. "But *when the fullness of the time came*, God sent forth His Son, born of a woman" (Galatians 4:4). Jesus referred to God's timing when He said, "My hour has not yet come" (John 2:4). In fact, no one was able to harm Jesus until it was time for Him to go to the cross. "... He taught in the temple; and no one seized Him, *because His hour had not yet come*" (John 8:20).

The Lord always knows the exact time He wants to answer each prayer. Solomon said, "There is an appointed time for everything. And there is a time for every event under heaven.... He has made everything appropriate in its time" (Ecclesiastes 3:1, 11). Although His scheduling is different for each situation, every now and then He will bring the answer sooner than we expect.

When my daughter Hannah was in grade school she wanted to join the Girl Scouts and needed a uniform. At that time I was pastor of a small church and was working a part-time job to make ends meet. I told her, "Hannah, why don't you pray and ask God for the uniform you need?"

She went into her bedroom and prayed for the Lord to provide it.

Two minutes later the phone rang. The woman on the other end of the phone said, "You don't know me, but I have a Girl Scout uniform that I would like to give away. Do you have a daughter who needs one?"

For a moment I held the phone in silence, as I was absolutely stunned. *Is this really happening?* I asked myself. *Just two minutes ago Hannah prayed for a uniform. This is impossible!*

I snapped out of it and answered, "Yes, we do have a daughter who needs a uniform. I know you might find this hard to believe, but she just prayed two minutes ago for a Girl Scout uniform, and then you called. Your phone call is an answer to my child's prayer."

Why did God answer her prayer so quickly? Maybe the Lord wanted to confirm to Hannah that He listens to her prayers. Perhaps the woman who called needed proof that He really exists. Maybe it was because He knew I would write about the incident in this book so it would inspire readers to pray about every need in their life.

What are the odds that a woman who didn't know us would call on the phone with the answer to Hannah's prayer just seconds later? The timing was just too incredible to be a coincidence. My daughter received the free uniform, which fit perfectly, from God.

It doesn't matter how long we've been waiting; God can still bring the answer.

The Lord typically doesn't answer prayers this swiftly. He usually takes much longer than we would like to bring us an answer. It might seem as though God doesn't care about our requests—that maybe He's too busy counting hairs on people's heads to be concerned about our needs.

God promised Abraham and Sarah they would have a child. Their answer didn't come until twenty-five years later. The Scripture tells us, "Without becoming weak in faith he contemplated his own body, now as good as dead since he was about a hundred years old, and the deadness of Sarah's womb; yet, with respect to the promise of God, he did not waver in unbelief but grew strong in faith, giving glory to God" (Romans 4:20–21). This proves that it doesn't matter how long we've been waiting; God can still bring the answer. He's not bound by time nor affected by it like we are.

When the answer is delayed and your situation is getting worse rather than better, you've got to keep trusting the Lord. "Waiting on the Lord" means there's an *unknown gap in time* between when you ask God for help and when His answer arrives. It's during this waiting period that you will be the most tempted to give up on God.

However, if you will be patient and continue to trust Him, your faith will grow and you'll actually become spiritually stronger. "Those who wait for the LORD will gain new strength. They will mount up with wings like eagles. They will run and not get tired. They will walk and not become weary" (Isaiah 40:31).

> "Waiting on the Lord" means there's an *unknown gap in time* between when you ask God for help and when His answer arrives.

WHY ANSWERS ARE DELAYED

Our son Scott called me on his cell phone, telling me that traffic had stopped on the interstate and he would be late arriving home. My wife started worrying and said, "I hope he'll be okay."

I told her, "There's nothing to worry about. It's just a delay."

My words caught me by surprise, as it seemed that God was repeating those words back to me. I had been waiting for the Lord to answer one of my prayers. It was as if He was saying, "There's nothing to worry about. It's just a delay." God's answers to our prayers can be delayed for three reasons.

REASON 1. WHAT YOU'RE PRAYING FOR MAY NOT BE READY.

God may require you to wait because the people and circumstances involved in His answer aren't ready. While you continue to pray and wait, the Lord is moving people around and changing circumstances to get things in place to answer your request. He's in the process of preparing what you're praying for, so you'll need to patiently wait for His perfect timing. When the time is right, all the players involved will converge beautifully at the right place.

Years ago when we planted a church in Kansas, we spent eleven years praying for land where we could construct a building. We thought we needed at least ten acres, and at that time land was selling for $45,000 per acre. We couldn't afford to buy ten acres at that price. Year after year we prayed and waited, but no door opened for us.

One day I prayed, "Lord, Walmart found land to build. Where is the land for your church?" Immediately the words "Eighth Street" came to my mind. Eighth Street was a long road of mostly farmland. I asked a realtor in our church to check out any property that might be for sale on Eighth Street.

During that same week, a member of our church came to me and said, "Pastor, I had a dream and saw our church was built on Eighth Street on the west side of the road." This surprised me because no one in the church knew that the realtor was looking for land on that street.

A few days later, the realtor reported, "Some property on Eighth Street just became available this week. People have been trying to buy this land for years, but it hasn't been for sale until now and the owners are willing to sell it to us at a reduced price." The land was in the exact location that the church member had seen in the dream!

For the eleven years when we had prayed for the Lord to provide land, this twenty-two acre property hadn't been for sale. But on the week the owners decided to sell it, God told us where it was. Although our prayers for property went on for years and years, the answer came suddenly. Instead of having to pay close to a million dollars for the land, it only cost us $55,000. We waited eleven long years for God to provide, and the waiting was well worth it. Because we bought the land at a bargain price, we were able to construct our church building debt free. When God's timing was right everything came together perfectly.

Perhaps you've been praying for years to meet the right person to marry.[8] You're frustrated because you haven't found the right person yet. First, be thankful that you haven't married the wrong person who would make your life miserable. After hearing what Jesus had to say about divorce, His disciples remarked that it was better to remain single (Matthew 19:10–11). In other words, even though being single can be lonely, it's less painful than going through the heartbreak of a divorce. Second, realize that God is the only one who knows who and where your future spouse is, and you must trust Him to bring you together. This requires that you don't panic as time passes, but that you believe in His sovereignty over your situation.

The Lord is more concerned about you receiving His best than about how quickly you can get it. God's timing is always right, even though we think our answer should always come as soon as possible. He often allows a waiting period to develop patience in us.

> The Lord is more concerned about
> you receiving His best than about
> how quickly you can get it.

REASON 2. SOMETHING IN THE SPIRITUAL REALM MAY BE DELAYING YOUR REQUEST.

The prophet Daniel was praying about the future of Israel when the angel Gabriel suddenly appeared to him (Daniel 9:20–21). This was over five hundred years before Gabriel appeared to Mary and Zacharias. Again, we see that angels know where to find us and that they continue to exist throughout the centuries. Gabriel explained to Daniel the prophetic timetable for when the Messiah would come.

After this, Daniel fasted and prayed for three weeks. At the end of that time, an unnamed angel appeared to him and explained the reason for his delay in coming:

> "Do not be afraid, Daniel, for *from the first day* that you set your heart on understanding this and on humbling yourself before your God, *your words were heard,* and I have come in response to your words. But the prince of the kingdom of Persia was withstanding me for twenty-one days; then behold, Michael, one of the chief princes, came to help me, for I had been left there with the kings of Persia." (Daniel 10:12–13)

Although we don't understand exactly what was happening in the spiritual realm, we do know *God heard his prayer on the first day he prayed.* However, the "prince of the kingdom of Persia," which was a demon that apparently influenced decisions made by the earthly king of Persia, kept the angel from visiting Daniel for three weeks. Michael the archangel came to help fight the demon so the angel could take this message to him:

> The angel said, "Do you understand why I came to you? But I shall now return to fight against the prince of Persia; so I am going forth, and behold, the prince of Greece is about to come." (Daniel 10:20)

This shows that there's a connection between the spiritual realm and earthly realm. The "princes" and "kings" of Persia and Greece were demons, representatives of Satan who had been assigned to those nations to fight against God's spiritual forces there and to try to influence events on earth.[9] History records that Persia was conquered by Greece, but at the time when the angel revealed this to Daniel, it had not happened yet. The warfare between these two earthly nations was in some way connected to the warfare happening in the spiritual realm. Daniel's prayers influenced the outcome of the war and the future destiny of Israel.

So if you think your prayers cannot make a difference, think again.

REASON 3. THE DELAY WILL HELP YOU APPRECIATE THE ANSWER WHEN IT COMES.

We usually appreciate a blessing more if we've been waiting for it for a long time. Delays force us to wait and trust Him to come through at the right time. We live in a world that wants *instant* gratification. But if we got everything instantly, we probably wouldn't appreciate what we receive. *Delayed* gratification means we're willing to say no to an immediate solution that isn't right, while patiently trusting God to provide a better answer at a later time.

As you're waiting, you might be tempted to provide for yourself illicitly—such as stealing or compromising your integrity. When the devil tempted Jesus in the wilderness, Satan tried to get Him to stop trusting His Father to provide, and use His own power to turn some stones into bread. "After He had fasted forty days and forty nights, He then became hungry. And the tempter came and said to Him, 'If You are the Son of God, command that these stones become bread'" (Matthew 4:2–3).

Notice it was *after* Jesus became hungry that the devil showed up to tempt His weakness. Satan knows that if you've been waiting for a long time for God to provide, it's easier to tempt you to take matters into your own hands and go after the wrong kind of provision. Satan will sometimes bring a wrong answer quickly so people will take it without thinking about the consequences. Those who want instant gratification will grab the quick provision—and will pay dearly for it later. God, on the other hand, is never in a hurry, but His answer will always be for our good and His glory.

Patience never loses sight of God's purposes. In the next chapter we'll see why we need to be persistent and keep praying as we wait.

10 | KNOCK, KNOCK

> "Yet because of his persistence he will get up
> and give him as much as he needs." (Luke 11:8)

Late one afternoon when the office was ready to close, the business manager finally allowed a life insurance salesman to see him. The manager told the salesman, "You should feel highly honored. Do you know that I have refused to see seven insurance men today?"

"I know," replied the salesman. "I'm them."

God loves to bless those who keep knocking after everyone else has clocked out and gone home. Because most people are looking for shortcuts, persistence is the most overlooked means of receiving God's blessings.

As we have seen, one of the purposes of prayer is to prove to God how badly we want something, which is where persistence comes in. Persistence gives us the determination to continue praying even when every difficult situation tempts us to stop. This is important because we never know exactly when God will answer our prayers. The timing is completely up to Him.

These three examples demonstrate what the Lord is looking for when we pray.

EXAMPLE 1—A GENTILE WOMAN WHO WON'T TAKE NO FOR ANSWER

A Canaanite woman asked Jesus to cast a demon out of her daughter. In response to her plea, "He did not answer her a word" (see Matthew 15:22–28). She could have become discouraged by His lack of response, thinking, "It must not be God's will," and turned around to go home.

The disciples wanted Jesus to send her away because she kept following them and shouting. He finally answered her, "I was sent only to the lost sheep of the house of Israel." Since she was a Gentile and not from Israel, it appeared as though Jesus was saying no to her.

She bowed down to Him and said, "Lord, help me!"

He told her, "It's not good to take the children's bread and throw it to the dogs."

No caring parent would take a meal away from their child and let the dog eat it. The "children" were the Israelites, and Gentiles were called dogs by the Jews. This appeared to be the final nail in the coffin for her request.

Rather than taking no for an answer, she replied, "Yes, Lord, but even the dogs feed on the crumbs which fall from their master's table." She wasn't asking to sit at the children's table to eat their food, but to crawl under the table and eat the crumbs they didn't want. Yes, she was a dog—a bulldog! She didn't need an entire meal but just one tiny crumb. She believed Jesus could miraculously heal her daughter as easily as He could turn water into wine.

Jesus wasn't trying to discourage her faith with His answers, but He was encouraging her faith to grow by letting her passionately pursue Him. Since she passed each test, Jesus told her, "O woman, your faith is great; it shall be done for you as you wish." And her daughter was immediately healed. She received her answer through her persistence in asking.

But what if she had quit asking after the first time? She wouldn't have received the answer. Instead, she kept going back to Jesus until she got her answer. Yes, it *was* God's will—because Jesus did heal her daughter.

Example 2—The parable of the friend at midnight

Jesus' disciples came to Him and said, "Lord, teach us to pray as John also taught his disciples" (Luke 11:1). In response to their request, Jesus told a parable about praying persistently:

"Suppose one of you has a friend, and goes to him at midnight and says to him, 'Friend, lend me three loaves; for a friend of mine has come to me from a journey, and I have nothing to set before him'; and from inside he answers and says, 'Do not bother me; the door has already been shut and my children and I are in bed. I cannot get up and give you anything.' I tell you, even though he will not get up and give him anything because he is his friend, yet because of his persistence he will get up and give him as much as he needs." (Luke 11:5–8)

The man came at midnight and started knocking at the door to ask for some bread. His friend would have helped him if he had come during the day, but not in the middle of the night. The neighbor didn't want to open the door because he wanted to stay in bed and get some sleep.

> Jesus teaches us how we can open
> closed doors by continuing to knock.

He didn't make up an excuse about not having any bread. He had plenty of food, since at the end of the parable it says he could "give him as much as he needs." His denial wasn't due to his lack of supplies, so the neighbor came up with a different excuse—"the door has already been shut." Denying his friend's request because the door had been shut is a picture of *a closed door* or obstacle that keeps us from getting what we need. In this parable, knocking is like our prayer request, while receiving the food is our answer from God. Jesus teaches us how we can open closed doors by continuing to knock persistently in prayer.

In those days people secured their houses by inserting a heavy bar through rings attached to the door. This door wasn't just closed, it was locked and barred. The bar had to be removed before it was possible for the door to open. How does a bolted door get unlocked? It must be opened *from the inside*. The friend inside the house had to change his mind and make a decision to unlock and open it.

The man's request was a prayer of intercession. Intercessory prayer means praying for someone else's need to be met. The person knocking on the door wasn't asking for bread for himself but was requesting it for his guest who had just arrived at his house from a journey.

His friend inside the house gave another excuse: "My children and I are in bed. I cannot get up and give you anything." Since the houses at that time were extremely small, the entire family would all sleep in the same room on different floor mats. The noise of unlocking the door would wake up the children.

The man at the door ignored these excuses and kept knock, knock, knocking away. One of the purposes of prayer is to show God how intensely we want something, and that's why we must keep knocking when we pray. Jesus concludes the parable: "I tell you, even though he will not get up and give him anything because he is his friend, yet *because of his persistence* he will get up and give him as much as he needs."

He finally answered the request but not because he was doing his friend a favor. The *only* reason for granting his wish was due to the man's continual pounding on the door. Persistence is the tireless determination to keep pursuing until you get what you need, which requires a never-give-up attitude. The man kept knocking on the door, knowing his friend wouldn't get any sleep until he answered the door and gave him what he wanted.

But what if he had quit knocking after the first refusal? He might have thought, "It must not be God's will," and returned home empty-handed. But it *was* God's will because he finally received the bread. Jesus explained that his persistent knocking brought the answer.

THREE KINDS OF KNOCKERS

Which type of person are you?

"IMMEDIATELY QUIT KNOCKING" PEOPLE

These people knock once and when the door doesn't immediately open, they assume that God has said, "Don't bother me." They reply, "Okay, Lord, sorry to bother You. I'll go home now. It must not have been Your will." They never knock a second time.

"GROW WEARY AND QUIT KNOCKING" PEOPLE

Some people start knocking but when the door doesn't open in their expected time frame, they assume that the answer must be no. They say, "If it was God's will, it would have happened by now."

One of the largest gold mines in the world was discovered just six inches deeper than the place where the last crew had quit digging. I believe many people would have received an answer to their prayer if they hadn't quit knocking so soon. Jesus, who answers our prayers, instructed us to not lose heart when we pray (Luke 18:1). He taught us that the correct way to pray is to be persistent, which is proof that we trust Him to answer in His timing.

"KNOCK UNTIL YOU RECEIVE" PEOPLE

These folks keep knocking and praying until the bread is in their hands. Many of God's blessings can only be received through great persistence. It was God's will for the man to receive the three loaves of bread, although it didn't look that way at first. He had to keep knocking for a while before the door opened and the bread was placed in his hands. The knocking process weeds out those who aren't serious about their request.

- Persistence eliminates merely *ritualistic* prayers—repeating the same words out of habit.

- Persistence eliminates *flippant* prayers—praying with no heart.

- Persistence eliminates *unbelieving* prayers—thinking that praying does no good.

The Lord earnestly desires to answer the prayers of those who have a burning desire in their hearts for their request—those who keep knocking until they get it.

How did the man know when to quit knocking? When his friend opened the door and gave him three loaves of bread. Not one loaf, and not even two loaves. Three. Jesus stated, "He will get up and *give him as much as he needs.*"

Scientists have proven the power of persistence through an experiment using an iron ball and a cork. In a lab experiment, a one-ton iron ball was suspended from the ceiling using a metal cable. A small cork was hung by a thread next to the heavy ball. An electrical mechanism kept the cork gently bouncing against the iron weight. After many days of constant pounding by the cork, the researchers were amazed to see the iron ball starting to move ever so slightly. The tiny cork continued to knock against it until the heavy ball swung widely back and forth on its own.[10]

When it looks like nothing is happening after you begin praying, remember that your persistence will be rewarded if you will keep knocking. Even the smallest prayers can be like the cork that slowly, persistently pushes the iron ball to move.

After He tells His disciples the parable about the persistent neighbor, the Master of prayer teaches His students how to pray: "And I say to you, ask, and it shall be given to you; seek, and you shall find; knock, and it shall be opened to you" (Luke 11:9). The present tense in the Greek text indicates continued action: "Keep on asking, keep on seeking, keep on knocking."

Some prayers are *asking* prayers—petitioning the Lord for provision.

Some are *seeking* prayers—pursuing God to show you what to do.

Some are *knocking* prayers—pounding on a locked door until it opens.

EXAMPLE 3—THE PARABLE OF THE UNJUST JUDGE AND THE WIDOW

Later Jesus told a different parable about prayer. This time, instead of asking from a friend, the person is requesting help from an atheistic, uncompassionate legal official.

Now He was telling them a parable to show that at all times they ought to pray and not to lose heart, saying, "In a certain city there was a judge who did not fear God and did not respect man. There was a widow in that city, and she kept coming to him, saying, 'Give me legal protection from my opponent.'

"For a while he was unwilling; but afterward he said to himself, 'Even though I do not fear God nor respect man, yet because this widow bothers me, I will give her legal protection, otherwise by continually coming she will wear me out.'"

And the Lord said, "Hear what the unrighteous judge said. Now, will not God bring about justice for His elect who cry to Him day and night, and will He delay long over them? I tell you that He will bring about justice for them quickly. However, when the Son of Man comes, will He find faith on the earth?" (Luke 18:1–8)

As Jesus teaches His disciples how prayer works, He instructs them to pray at all times and not to get discouraged and quit praying. It's easy for us to become discouraged when we don't see an immediate answer, so He specifically instructs us to keep pressing on and not to be deterred.

Jesus taught by using two different kinds of parables. A parable of *comparison* shows the similarities between one thing and another. For example, Jesus said, "The kingdom of heaven is *like* a treasure hidden in the field" (Matthew 13:44). A parable of *contrast* shows the differences between one thing and another. In this type of parable, Jesus tells a story about an unrighteous person to make a point that we might not otherwise grasp. An example is the parable of the unrighteous steward (Luke 16:1–12), where we learn about using our money for eternal purposes.

The parable of the unrighteous judge takes us into the legal system and introduces two people at opposite ends of the spectrum. The judge was seated in the position of authority and had little fear of opposition. He had no sense of personal accountability to God for his actions, nor was he troubled by sensitivity to those in need.

On the other end of the spectrum was a poor, helpless widow, who had no clout in that society. After her husband died, since she had no protector or advocate, an unscrupulous person had exploited her for what little she had. Although her concern seemed miniscule in others' eyes, the small amount she lost was extremely valuable to her. This is a significant part of the parable because what we are asking God for might seem trivial to others, but is precious to us. But even with justice on her side, the legal system wouldn't help her with an indifferent judge.

Most people are motivated to help others for two reasons. One reason is a person's conscience toward God and the other is their compassion for others. Jesus sets up this parable by eliminating these two primary reasons the judge might have been moved to help her. And this leaves only one other weapon she could use—her determination.

Jesus explains this about the judge: "For a while he was unwilling." When the widow first started asking, he kept telling her no. She could have thought, "It must not be God's will," and stopped pleading with him. Although the poor widow didn't see an immediate approval of her request, she kept approaching him anyway. The judge grew tired of seeing her come and told himself, "Because this widow bothers me, I will give her legal protection, otherwise by continually coming she will wear me out."

The ungodly judge changed his mind and granted her plea for only one reason—she wouldn't stop bringing her request to him. She refused to take no for an answer. Jesus paints this picture to show us that *He wants us to have this kind of persistence when we pray*. We must continue praying until we receive an answer or until the Lord changes our hearts to pray differently. And if we are convinced in our hearts that the answer is on its way, we can shift our focus from asking Him to thanking Him.

For this reason Jesus told this parable of contrast: If an evil judge will answer this widow's request through her persistence, then how much more will a generous, compassionate God answer His children who "cry to Him day and night" (Luke 18:7)? "Cry out" expresses the urgency in our hearts, while "day and night" shows our determination over time. Elsewhere in the Scripture we are encouraged to "[be] imitators of those who through faith and patience inherit the promises" (Hebrews 6:12). It takes both faith and patience to persistently come before God in prayer.

> We must continue praying until we
> receive an answer or until the Lord
> changes our hearts to pray differently.

Jesus asks a puzzling question at the end of the parable. "However, when the Son of Man comes, will He find faith on the earth?" Jesus is challenging His followers to endure in prayer. The issue isn't the goodness of God, but our willingness to persevere. God isn't like the unjust judge, but are we like the determined widow? We can trust Him to answer, but can He trust us to keep asking?

PRAYER

Heavenly Father, thank you that you love me and only want the best for me. I believe that you hear my prayers and it's your desire to answer. Forgive me when I get impatient and discouraged while waiting for your answer to be manifest. I choose to be persistent in my prayers as I patiently wait for your perfect will and timing in my situation. I trust you and will give you praise when the answer becomes reality. In Jesus' name.

11 | HOW HEAVEN SEES PRAYERS

"Their voice was heard and their prayer
came to His holy dwelling place, to
heaven." (2 Chronicles 30:27)

When I was young, one particular scene in the movie *The Wizard of Oz* scared the wits out of me. Dorothy, the scarecrow, the tin man, and the cowardly lion are permitted to enter the Wizard's throne room. Fire and smoke surround the throne.

The cowardly lion sees the fire and smoke and is absolutely terrified. He starts crying, "*I want to go home!*" A huge image of the Wizard's head floats up before them and says in a booming voice, "I am Oz, the great and powerful! Who are you?"

The fearful four tremble in the Wizard's presence. Dorothy timidly steps forward and says to the big face of the Wizard, "If you please, I'm Dorothy. We've come to ask you . . ."

With lights flashing on and off, the stern Wizard interrupts her with a thundering, "Silence! The great and powerful Oz knows why you have come." He then tells the tin man, "You *dare* to come to me for a heart, do you? You clinking, clanking, clattering collection of junk!"

This is how some people envision God on His throne in heaven when they pray. They view Him as an angry wizard who cannot be bothered with their requests. Nothing could be further from the truth.

What Happens When You Pray?

When you put a letter in your mailbox, you probably don't think about how it gets to its destination. All you know is that you must make sure you have the correct address on the letter, or the intended recipient won't get it. But if you followed that letter, you would discover it takes many workers, machines, and vehicles to handle your mail to get it to the right person.

If you want your prayer to reach heaven, you must address it to the one true God. But what happens after that? You may never have thought about how your prayer ascends into heaven and arrives at God's throne.

A Roman centurion named Cornelius was a Gentile who gave alms to the Jewish people and continually prayed to God. One afternoon an angel appeared to him and said, "Cornelius, your prayers and alms have ascended as a memorial before God" (Acts 10:4). Wouldn't it be great to have an angel appear every time you prayed to let you know your prayer had been heard by God?

What was the purpose of this unexpected angelic visitation? Cornelius was not a Jew, so he probably wondered if his prayers were being heard by the God of Israel. The angel revealed to him that his prayers and contributions in the earthly realm had ascended into the heavenly realm to the Lord. Never forget that whenever you pray and give your offerings, it doesn't stop here on earth, but is instantly brought into heaven before God's throne.

In the book of Revelation, we get a glimpse into the spiritual realm of heaven. Revelation 5:8 tells us that in heaven the prayers of the saints are put in golden bowls full of incense. These prayers aren't from those who worship a different god, but are the prayers of "all the saints" (8:3). A "saint" isn't a deceased righteous person as some believe, but is anyone who believes in the Lord Jesus Christ and is cleansed by His blood (1 Corinthians 1:2; Ephesians 1:1). The following passage describes how the smoke from the incense, along with the saints' prayers, ascended before God:

Another angel came and stood at the altar, holding a golden censer; and much incense was given to him, so that he might add it to the *prayers of all the saints* on the golden altar which was before the throne. And the *smoke of the incense, with the prayers of the saints*, went up before God out of the angel's hand. (Revelation 8:3–4)

To correctly interpret this passage we must understand the function of the altar of incense in the Old Testament tabernacle. The Lord told Moses to build the tabernacle to be an exact replica of the one in heaven. The tabernacle served as a "copy and shadow of *the heavenly things*" (Hebrews 8:5). God wanted him to construct it exactly as He specified because the earthly tabernacle would be used as a prototype that would teach us about what would transpire in heaven.

In the Old Testament tabernacle and temple, the most important ritual took place at the "mercy seat," or the lid that covered the Ark of the Covenant, which contained the Ten Commandments. The breaking of these commandments would bring God's judgment, unless He showed mercy by allowing someone to make atonement. On the Day of Atonement, the high priest sprinkled goat's blood on the mercy seat in the holy place. This atoned for the people's sins and demonstrated that "mercy triumphs over judgment" when the blood is applied to the mercy seat (James 2:13).

This annual ritual, performed by the high priest, was designed by God to teach the people of Israel how Jesus the Messiah would sprinkle His own blood on the mercy seat in heaven (Hebrew 12:24). After His crucifixion, the book of Hebrews explains, "He entered through the *greater and more perfect tabernacle, not made with hands*, that is to say, not of this creation; and not through the blood of goats and calves, but through His own blood, *He entered the holy place* once for all, having obtained eternal redemption" (Hebrews 9:11–12).

Placing blood on the earthly mercy seat was an object lesson to help us understand how Jesus atoned for our sins by placing His blood on the heavenly mercy seat. We would have never known about how Christ purchased our eternal salvation with His blood in heaven if we hadn't known about this ritual done by the Old Testament high priest.

Just as it prepared the people to understand Jesus' heavenly atonement, the earthly tabernacle was also designed to teach us how God receives prayer in heaven. In Revelation 8:3, the "golden altar" which is before God's throne corresponds to the Old Testament altar of incense. In the earthly tabernacle and temple, this altar was located in front of the veil nearest to the mercy seat, which was the place of God's presence (Exodus 30:6; Leviticus 16:2).

The incense used in the temple was a sweet smelling perfume composed of four spices (Exodus 30:34–38). When the priest burned incense, it created the most pleasing aroma imaginable. King David told the Lord, "May my prayer be counted as incense before You" (Psalm 141:2). The smoke from the altar of incense symbolized the prayers of His people ascending into God's presence and His acceptance of them. William Barclay writes, "The idea is that prayer is a sacrifice to God. The prayers of the saints are offered on the altar, and like all other sacrifices, they are surrounded with the perfume of the incenses as they rise to God."[11]

Again, this ritual in the earthly tabernacle served as an object lesson to help us understand prayer from heaven's perspective. Dr. John Walvoord writes:

> In [Revelation 8:3] another angelic personage is introduced as standing before the altar with a golden censer presenting incense and the prayers of the saints before the throne. *This is a beautiful picture of the prayers of the saints as seen from heaven.* In the Old Testament order the priests would burn incense on the altar of incense, and the smoke would fill the Temple or Tabernacle and would then ascend to heaven. Incense was symbolic of worship and prayer, and a reminder that intercession to the Lord has the character of sweet incense.[12]

Why does Revelation describe the angel adding incense to our prayers in heaven? To show that they are pleasing and acceptable to God. Lest you get the wrong idea, this isn't cheap incense that's burned to cover up odors, but a valuable and pleasant perfume. When people go to a public place, such as a nice restaurant, they will put on perfume because they want others to smell the pleasing fragrance. When we pray according to the will of God, it's a pleasant fragrance to Him, like smelling expensive perfume.

As we saw in a previous chapter, it was no accident that the angel appeared to Zacharias in the temple on the right side of the *altar of incense*, which was where incense was burned and prayers were offered to God. Did the angel leave the altar of incense in heaven to appear at the altar of incense on earth? Apparently so. The angel said, "I am Gabriel, who stands *in the presence of God*" (Luke 1:19). Gabriel announced that Zacharias' prayer had been accepted by God in heaven, even though he hadn't yet seen the answer manifested on earth.

The Throne of Grace, Not the Throne of Terror

In Revelation 8:3, the prayers of all the saints are on the golden altar that is *before the throne*, which is also known as "the throne of grace." God answers our prayers from His throne in heaven. The writer of Hebrews tells us, "Let us therefore come boldly to the throne of grace, that we may obtain mercy and find grace to help in time of need" (Hebrews 4:16 NKJV). This verse tells us five things about the throne of grace—who, where, how, why, and when.

> God hears every prayer of every believer in the entire world—and knows how to answer each one individually.

1. WHO can go—"Let us therefore come"

Who is "us" in this verse? Does this mean anyone who prays can go to the throne of grace, or is "us" limited to a certain group of people? Anyone who wants to be saved, or has been saved, can come to the throne of grace. Hebrews 4:14 says, "Therefore, since we have a great high priest who has passed through the heavens, Jesus the Son of God, let us hold fast our confession." God hears every prayer of every believer in the entire world—and knows how to answer each one individually.

2. WHERE TO GO—"TO THE THRONE OF GRACE"

I would be petrified if God named His throne "the throne of terror." Instead of a scepter to bless people, He would use a lightning bolt to zap them! I would never want to pray if I had to go before a throne by that name. But the Lord named it "the throne of grace" to give us confidence so we would feel welcome when we approach Him. Grace is a warm invitation to come before His throne.

In the cartoon *Dennis the Menace,* Dennis and his friend Joey are walking away from the Wilsons' house with their hands full of cookies. Joey asks, "I wonder what we did to deserve this?" Dennis replies, "Look Joey, Mrs. Wilson gives us cookies—not because we're nice, but because she's nice."

God's grace proceeds from God's goodness. And He meets our needs, not because we're good, but because He's good. That's why it's called the throne of *grace.*

3. HOW TO GO—"COME BOLDLY"

God invites us to come boldly before His throne of grace. The Greek word for *boldly* means "to speak confidently without fear." We can come into His presence and ask for whatever we need without the fear of being rejected.

Jesus' last words before He died on the cross were, "Father, into your hands I commit my spirit" (Luke 23:46). At that moment, Jesus *in His spirit* (not His body) went to heaven and sprinkled His blood on the mercy seat in the heavenly temple (Hebrews 9:11–12). This action in heaven became evident on earth when "the veil of the temple was torn in two from top to bottom" (Matthew 27:51).

This veil, which separated the Holy of Holies from the rest of the temple, was sixty feet high and four inches thick, and could not have been torn by human hands. But God ripped it in half "from top to bottom" to demonstrate that this action came from heaven, and to open the Holy of Holies. Up until then, only the high priest could go behind the curtain, but removing the veil opened the way for all believers to enter the presence of God.

The seat of mercy has become the throne of grace. We can now come boldly to the throne of grace, not because of our own righteousness, but because Jesus atoned for our sins with His blood. We can come boldly before God because He's torn down the veil of separation and we're on the same side.

The seat of mercy has become the throne of grace.

---

4. WHY TO GO—"THAT WE MAY OBTAIN MERCY AND FIND GRACE TO HELP"

We can have confidence to bring our requests to God because He wants to help us whenever we are in trouble. "God is our refuge and strength, always ready to help in times of trouble" (Psalm 46:1 NLT).

We will receive two things when we come before His throne—mercy and grace. Mercy is the heart of God, and grace is the hand of God. Mercy is not getting what we deserve. Grace is getting what we don't deserve.

When people called out to Jesus for mercy, He gave grace to help them.

- Two blind men cried out, "Have mercy on us," and Jesus healed them (Matthew 9:27).

- A Canaanite woman cried out, "Have mercy on me," and Jesus healed her daughter (Matthew 15:22).

- A man cried out, "Have mercy on my son," and Jesus healed him (Matthew 17:15).

- Ten lepers shouted, "Have mercy on us," and all were healed (Luke 17:13).

At the throne we find *grace to help* us, which is the answer to our prayers. "From where shall my help come? My help comes from the LORD, who made heaven and earth" (Psalm 121:1–2). The Lord will intervene in the situation that concerns us, or He will give us grace to endure the problem we face. Hebrews 13:9 says, "[I]t is good for the heart to be strengthened by grace." Grace gives us power to press on when we cannot go on in our own strength.

5. WHEN TO GO—"IN TIME OF NEED"

Sometimes we don't have an urgent need, but at other times we do. God promises to help us in our *time* of need. Whenever you have a need, it's time to go to the throne of grace. The Lord is aware of your situation and will help you get through it.

When Corrie ten Boom, author of *The Hiding Place*, was a little girl in Holland, she was afraid of dying. Corrie's father comforted her with words of wisdom. "Corrie, when you and I go to Amsterdam, when do I give you your train ticket?"

"Just before I get on the train," Corrie replied.

"Exactly," her father said. "I hold your ticket for you and then give it to you just before you get on the train. Our wise Father in heaven knows when you're going to need things too. Don't run out ahead of Him, Corrie. When the time comes to die, you will look into your heart and find the strength you need—just in time."

Now you understand how heaven sees prayer and why you can joyfully come before God's throne in your time of need.

12 | "IN JESUS' NAME" DOESN'T MEAN "SINCERELY YOURS"

"God highly exalted Him, and bestowed
on Him the name which is above every
name, so that at the name of Jesus every
knee will bow." (Philippians 2:9–10)

"Sincerely yours." It's a nice way to end your correspondence. But have you ever thought about what "sincerely yours" or "yours truly" actually means? Most people can't tell you. It's just something nearly everyone has written before signing their name.

"Sincerely" means totally honest. "Yours" means you're giving yourself totally to the other person. But you must admit that you're not always sincere—and you're not giving yourself and all you own to that other person. "Sincerely yours" has come to mean "this letter is about to end."

We typically end our prayers by saying "In Jesus' name" as a nice way to close a prayer. We use it as a "sincerely yours," or "This is what I always say just before amen." Most people cannot tell you what "In Jesus' name" means, or why we include it in our prayers.

THE RIGHT TO USE HIS NAME

When a man and woman are dating, what they each own is separated under their different names. But when they get married, they are legally joined together by covenant and they often share the same last name. Now whatever one of them owned also belongs to the other, and they each have full access to it.

When you trust Jesus to be your Lord, you are joined together with Him by covenant. "And there is salvation in no one else; for there is *no other name* under heaven that has been given among men by which we must be saved" (Acts 4:12). As part of the covenant, Jesus gives you the right to use His name when you pray. He said, "You did not choose Me but I chose you, and appointed you that you would go and bear fruit, and that your fruit would remain, so that whatever you ask of the Father *in My name* He may give to you" (John 15:16).

You must be in covenant with Him before you have the authority to use His name. Some people, who are not true believers in Him, will try to invoke His name to cast out demons and perform miracles. On the Judgment Day their hypocrisy will be exposed. Jesus said, "Many will say to Me on that day, 'Lord, Lord, did we not prophesy *in Your name*, and *in Your name* cast out demons, and *in Your name* perform many miracles?' And then I will declare to them, 'I never knew you; DEPART FROM ME, YOU WHO PRACTICE LAWLESS-NESS'" (Matthew 7:22–23).

Notice that they will "say" they did these things, although they didn't actually do them. Jesus tells them, "I never knew you," so they had no right to use His name.

What Does "In Jesus' Name" Really Mean?

A little girl went to her next door neighbor and asked for some sugar. The neighbor denied her request. The next day the girl's mother was cooking and ran out of sugar. She sent her daughter next door to borrow some, and this time neighbor gave her a cup full.

The girl asked, "Why did you give me sugar today when you wouldn't yesterday?"

"Yesterday you asked for yourself," the neighbor explained, "but today you asked in your mother's name."

When we pray, we don't come to the Father in our own name, but in the name of His Son. Asking in the name of Jesus can be understood through the following three terms.

1. "BY THE AUTHORITY OF"

"In the name of" means "by the delegated authority of." A higher authority designates someone to use their authority. When a policeman says, "Stop in the name of the law," he's announcing that he represents the law and can use its authority to make you stop if you refuse to obey.

Jesus explained that He did miracles because He received delegated authority from His Father. He said, "I told you, and you do not believe; the works that I do *in My Father's name*, these testify of Me" (John 10:25). His ability to do miracles was connected to His Father's name.

In those days when a king sent a representative on a mission, that person received delegated authority from the king. Jesus sent out seventy disciples into cities where He had planned to go in the near future. When they returned, they said, "Lord, even the demons are subject to us in Your name" (Luke 10:17). The disciples were amazed that they could cast out demons using Jesus' name. It wasn't by their own power that they performed miracles, but by the authority that had been delegated to them by Jesus.

"In the name of" means you are acting for someone else as their representative. If your boss asks you to call another company and says, "Tell them that I told you to call," you're calling them in your boss's name. When they talk to you, it carries the same weight as if they were talking with your boss. Jesus said, "Whoever receives this child in My name receives Me, and *whoever receives Me receives Him who sent Me*" (Luke 9:48).

2. "ACCORDING TO GOD'S WILL"

Praying in Jesus' name means asking according to His will, which means you must first submit your will to His. "This is the confidence which we have before Him, that, if we ask anything according to His will, He hears us. And if we know that He hears us in whatever we ask, we know that we have the requests which we have asked from Him" (1 John 5:14–15). When we ask for something that is in God's will, we can have confidence that He already desires to give it to us.

Some people are afraid that they will ask for something that isn't God's will. And so whenever they pray, they always add, "If it be Thy will, God." In the Garden of Gethsemane, Jesus pleaded with His Father to let the cup of suffering pass by Him. He prayed, "My Father, if it is possible, let this cup pass from Me; yet not as I will, but as You will" (Matthew 26:39).

This was the only time He prayed those words. Jesus knew He was destined to die on the cross for the sins of the world, but in His humanity He wanted to be spared from the agony. Yet Jesus also wanted His Father's plan to be done over His own desire.

It's absolutely right to ask God to give you the same attitude Jesus had in Gethsemane. We should always want to remain in God's will, so that we can represent His kingdom. No king would grant anyone the use of his name without first being assured that his will would be done through that representative. Followers of Jesus Christ are citizens of His kingdom: "For our citizenship is in heaven" (Philippians 3:20). "We are ambassadors for Christ, *as though God were making an appeal through us*" (2 Corinthians 5:20). An ambassador is a representative appointed by one country to represent it in another. God has sent us as ambassadors from His kingdom into this present world to represent Him.

When an ambassador is sent on an assignment to another country, she can use her king's name to conduct business. She doesn't go on the assignment to do whatever she wants, but acts according to the king's wishes. On the other hand, the ambassador doesn't call the king to ask permission every time she needs to be make a decision:

"Hello, Your Highness, this is your ambassador. I have a question. Is it your will for me to put cream in my coffee, or do you want me to drink it black? I don't want to do anything against your will. I like cream but if it's not your will, I'll deny myself. . . . You say that you don't care? Well, okay then. I have one more question. Is it your will for me to wear my red dress or the black one? . . . You say that it doesn't matter? Well, okay."

The king has already authorized her to do business on his behalf. Because she knows his desire in most situations, there's no need to keep asking his permission. However, if a major situation is unclear, then the ambassador might call the king to get clarification.

Jesus gives us His name to use without spelling out every detail about how and when to use it. He gives us great freedom to ask in His name with confidence. "If you ask Me *anything in My name*, I will do it" (John 14:14). When we pray, it's understood that we always want God's will to override our will if we are asking incorrectly. The Holy Spirit will intercede and correct our intentions according to the will of God.

As long as we are seeking God, we don't need to always say, "If it be Thy will" in every prayer. We'll know God's will through His Word and the Holy Spirit bearing witness with our spirit. "The Spirit Himself bears witness with our spirit that we are children of God" (Romans 8:16 NKJV).

> When we pray, it's understood that we always want God's will to override our will if we are asking incorrectly.

3. "In the account of"

If I go to the bank and ask to withdraw money from my account, I'm asking for the money *in my name.* However, if I go to the bank with a check that you've signed and addressed to me, then I'm asking *in your name.* For me to receive the money in your name, several things are necessary.

First, you must have more money in your account than the amount on the check. If you don't have enough money, the check cannot be cashed.

Second, you must sign your name on the check. Your signature verifies that you are permitting me to take money out of your account.

Third, I must choose to cash your check. The amount of cash on the check is potentially mine, but the transaction must be completed by signing my name on the back of your check. Even though you've authorized the money for me, if I don't cash the check and receive the money, it's not mine.

Following this analogy, when I pray it's as if I'm making a transaction with the bank of heaven. I can make a request to the Father for what I need by asking in Jesus' name. Jesus said, "Truly, truly, I say to you, if you *ask the Father* for anything *in My name*, He will give it to you. Until now you have asked for nothing in My name; ask and you will receive, so that your joy may be made full" (John 16:23–24). He wants us to receive answers to our prayers so that our joy may be made full. Don't overlook this important fact—the Lord is pleased when His children are filled with joy because a prayer has been answered.

Jesus has promised us, "Whatever you ask in My name, that will I do, so that the Father may be glorified in the Son. If you ask Me anything in My name, I will do it" (John 14:13–14). And when your prayer is answered, don't forget to thank Him so that your Father in heaven is glorified.

PRAYER

Heavenly Father, I come to you in the name of Jesus and I ask you for (*name your request*). I know that it's only by the authority Jesus has given me that I have the right to make this request. And when you answer my prayer, I will give you all the credit so that you will be glorified. In Jesus' name.

13 | GOD WANTS TO SPEAK TO YOU

"Today if you hear His voice, do not
harden your hearts." (Hebrews 4:7)

I once had an appointment to meet with a businesswoman about a
matter. I had traveled to her city and only had an hour to visit with
her. When we sat down at the restaurant, she started talking with
the rapidity of an auctioneer about everything going on in her life.
It didn't take me long to realize that I might not have a chance to
say anything.

I didn't want to be rude and interrupt her, so I sat back and listened to her talk non-stop. I kept waiting for her to take a breath . . .
to pause . . . to hesitate ever so slightly so I could get a word in edge-
wise, but she never gave me the opportunity. At the end of the hour
she was still talking when it was time for me to leave. I said, "I hate
to interrupt you, but I need to go to my other scheduled appointment. Thank you so much for your time. It was nice talking to you."

Although she might not have realized it, I never did talk to her
because she didn't allow me the opportunity. Unfortunately, this is
how many people pray. They only talk to God and never even consider the fact that He might want to say something to them.

The primary purpose of prayer is to have a dialogue with God.
But if we don't expect Him to speak to us, we're only giving a mono-
logue and missing what He wants to say to us. I can't have a dialogue
with someone if I'm the only one talking.

Jesus said, "My sheep *hear My voice*, and I know them, and they follow Me" (John 10:27). The "sheep" are His followers, and Jesus said we will hear His voice speaking to us. God does want to speak to you. I have heard from Him many times as I've sought His face.

One day as I was praying I said, "Lord, this universe is so huge and I'm so small. Why would you want to speak to me?" Immediately the thought came to my mind, *I don't want to only speak with you. I want to talk to everyone else in the world, too.*

As strange as it sounds, I had never thought about that before. I knew that He wants to speak to His followers, but what about all the people who hate Him? Yes, God would like to speak to everyone He has created, but many people don't believe in Him, or they don't want to hear what He has to say. Yet there is another reason some people don't hear His voice. They hold to a theology that asserts that the Lord doesn't speak to people today. Before we can discuss how He speaks, we must address this doctrinal issue that has caused many people to doubt God's ability to communicate with His people today.

DOES GOD ONLY SPEAK THROUGH THE BIBLE?

You've probably heard of the Great Brink's Robbery. On January 17, 1950, a team of eleven thieves stole $2.7 million from the Brink's Armored Car depot in Boston. At the time, it was the largest robbery in the history of the United States. All eleven members of the gang were later arrested. But the real Great Brink's Robbery is when you're on the brink of a blessing and someone interprets it away. There's a sure way to make certain that this doesn't happen to you. The Holy Spirit, who inspired the Scriptures, will help you interpret passages correctly (see 2 Peter 1:20–21).

Some people believe God doesn't speak individually to people today because we have the entire Bible to read. They presuppose that the Lord only speaks through the Bible and that it's the only way He communicates with His people. By making this incorrect assumption, they conclude that any revelation outside the Bible cannot be from God.

However, reading the Bible doesn't guarantee that He will speak to you through it or that you will hear His voice. Even though the Pharisees continually studied and memorized the Scriptures, Jesus told them, "You have [not] heard His voice at any time. . . . You search the Scriptures because *you think that in them* you have eternal life. . . ." (John 5:37, 39). They never heard God speak to them through the Scriptures or in any other way, for that matter.

Adherents for this man-made doctrine, which teaches that God doesn't speak today, usually base their arguments on this Scripture: "For we know in part and prophesy in part, but when the perfect comes, the partial will be done away" (1 Corinthians 13:9–10). This interpretation assumes that "the perfect" in this verse refers to the Bible, meaning that Christians didn't need any further information from God once the complete New Testament had been written. But while it's certainly true that the Scriptures are God's recorded revelation to us, that doesn't mean He is limited to speaking only through them. If you have been taught this theology, would you please carefully consider these six problems with that interpretation of 1 Corinthians 13:9–10?

Problem 1. Nowhere in the Scriptures does it prophesy that a Bible will be written. An important principle in interpreting the Scriptures is to read the passage for what it actually says and *not what you think* it says. The phrase has been translated by Greek scholars as "when the perfect comes" and not "when the Bible is written and completed." Replacing the word "perfect" with the word "Bible" is altering the Scriptures for the sole purpose of substantiating a particular theology.

Problem 2. God does speak through the words in the Bible, but that does not exclude Him from also speaking information to our minds. This does not mean that additional Scriptures or other books can be added to the Bible. It simply means the Scriptures give general instructions to everyone, but the Holy Spirit can give specific guidance to each individual concerning what to do in their unique situations. The Holy Spirit will never speak in a way that contradicts the written Word, which He inspired.

Problem 3. The meaning of "when the perfect comes" is found a couple of verses later: "For now we see in a mirror dimly, but then face to face; now I know in part, but then I shall *know fully* just as I also have been fully known" (1 Corinthians 13:12). Does anyone on earth "know fully," even if they have memorized every word in the Bible? Of course not. "Face to face" means when we stand face to face with Jesus in eternity. If "the perfect" meant the Bible, it would say "face to page." When we stand face to face with Him in heaven one day, then our knowledge will be expanded and we will know completely just as we have been completely known by the Lord.

Problem 4. Claiming that God only speaks through the Bible contradicts many other Scriptures, particularly those concerning the role of the Holy Spirit. If you believe the Bible is God's Word, then you must also acknowledge that it is *from the Scriptures* that we learn that the Holy Spirit will speak to us. Jesus told us what the Holy Spirit would do:

> I have many more things to say to you, but you cannot bear them now. But when He, the Spirit of truth, comes, He will guide you into all the truth; for He will not speak on His own initiative, but whatever He hears, *He will speak*; and *He will disclose to you* what is to come. (John 16:12–13)

Why would Jesus tell us the Holy Spirit would speak to us if He cannot speak to us today? Are we to believe what Jesus taught, or should we believe a man-invented theology that insists God doesn't speak to us today? That idea denies what Jesus clearly taught, which is revealed in the Scriptures!

Problem 5. To maintain that the Lord only speaks through the Scriptures assumes that every word God says must be recorded in the Scriptures. But this isn't true. God spoke many messages through prophets in Old Testament times, but most of those words aren't recorded in the Bible.

Then Saul sent messengers to take David, but when they saw the company of the prophets prophesying, with Samuel standing and presiding over them, the *Spirit of God came upon the messengers of Saul; and they also prophesied.* (1 Samuel 19:20)

Even though the Spirit of God spoke words through them, we don't know exactly what they said because it's not recorded in the Scriptures. The Lord also spoke through the prophet Agabus in the New Testament about a coming famine (Acts 11:28), but his exact words aren't written in the Bible. Not even all the words of Jesus are recorded in the Scriptures. He said:

"I did not speak on My own initiative, but the Father Himself who sent Me has given Me a commandment as to *what to say and what to speak . . .* therefore the things I speak, *I speak just as the Father has told Me.*" (John 12:49–50)

The Father spoke through Jesus and yet many of those words are not recorded in the Scriptures. The apostle John wrote in his Gospel that Jesus performed many miracles, and obviously spoke many words, which are not recorded:

Therefore many other signs Jesus also performed in the presence of the disciples, which are not written in this book. . . . And there are also many other things which Jesus did, which if they were written in detail, I suppose that even the world itself would not contain the books that would be written. (John 20:30, 21:25)

Are we to assume that since Jesus' miracles are not recorded, He didn't do them? Or that since not all His words are written in the Bible, they weren't from God? Certainly not. This proves God can speak personal messages to individuals.

Problem 6. In His confrontation with the devil, Jesus quotes the Old Testament Scripture, "Man shall not live on bread alone, but on *every word that proceeds out of the mouth of God*" (Matthew 4:4). The doctrine that God only speaks through the Bible places a restriction of the Lord's desire to communicate with us and eliminates much of what He wants to say.

The Bible tells us that we can ask God for wisdom and He will give it (James 1:5). Why would you pray for wisdom if every answer could be found by reading the Bible? Why would you pray for wisdom if your belief system dictated that the Lord doesn't speak to us today? (Can you see how this non-Scriptural doctrine prevents people from seeking God's help?) James isn't talking about reading the Bible, but about receiving insights and guidance from the Lord about what to do in specific situations. This will be addressed in detail in an upcoming chapter.

How Does God Speak to Us?

God's written Word is the clearest revelation through which He will speak, so we need to spend time reading it every day. Many of the answers you are looking for are found in the pages of the Bible. But the Holy Spirit was sent to speak to us concerning issues not mentioned in the Bible. God's Word gives *general* guidance to everyone, but the Holy Spirit can give you *specific* guidance concerning your present-day situation. The Bible can tell you to marry a Christian, but the Holy Spirit can lead you to the right person to marry. The guidance of the Spirit will always be in harmony with God's Word.

> God's Word gives *general* guidance to everyone, but the Holy Spirit can give you *specific* guidance concerning your present-day situation.

So then, how does He speak? Occasionally God speaks to people in an audible voice from heaven, such as when Jesus was baptized (see Mark 1:11), when He was transfigured on the mountain (see Matthew 17:5) and when Saul heard Him speak in Hebrew on the road to Damascus (see Acts 26:14). The Lord spoke to Samuel in an audible voice and gave him a message to tell Eli the priest (see

1 Samuel 3). When David asked God, "Shall I go up against the Philistines?" the Lord answered, "Go up, for I will certainly give the Philistines into your hand" (2 Samuel 5:19). The Lord communicated to him by giving clear and specific instructions.

However, speaking in an audible voice is not His normal way of communicating with us today. The Lord doesn't need to use a human voice to speak to us. He can communicate with us by putting thoughts and ideas in our minds. In addition to the Scriptures, the Lord can speak to us in these three ways.

The Lord doesn't need to use a human voice to speak to us.

---

1. GOD CAN SPEAK THROUGH THOUGHTS IN YOUR MIND.

God communicates to us through thoughts and ideas that He speaks to our minds. Jesus once asked His disciples, "Who do you say that I am?" Peter answered, "You are the Christ, the Son of the living God" (Matthew 15:16–17). How did Peter know this fact about Jesus' identity? He probably thought that he came up with that idea on his own. But Jesus informed him that His Father in heaven had revealed His identity as the Son of God to Peter. The Lord spoke to Peter by putting the idea into his mind (see Matthew 16:13–17).

When God directed Nehemiah to go to Jerusalem and rebuild the city wall, he said, "I did not tell anyone what my *God was putting in my mind* to do for Jerusalem" (Nehemiah 2:12). The entire plan began with the Lord planting thoughts into his mind. After the wall was built, Nehemiah said, "*God put it into my heart* to assemble the nobles" (Nehemiah 7:5). The Lord communicated what He wanted done by putting thoughts in Nehemiah's mind and heart.

Jesus said the Holy Spirit "will disclose to you what is to come" (John 16:13). Because He knows the future, He is able to guide us and reveal to us "what is to come."

Several years ago, the Lord revealed to my wife Cindy something that was about to happen. Cindy was praying on a Wednesday as she watered the bushes in our yard. A thought popped into her mind saying, *Someone is going to give you a car.* Those words seemed to come out of nowhere, but Cindy knew it was the Lord speaking to her. A newer vehicle was something we really needed.

The next evening, a couple we had recently met invited us to their house for dinner on Friday. After we finished dining with them, the couple surprised us by announcing, "The Lord has spoken to us that we are to give you a car. It's a PT Cruiser, only a couple of years old, and we'd like for you to have it. Has the Lord given you any confirmation on this?"

Cindy instantly recalled the words she heard two days earlier. She said, "Yes. I was in my backyard on Wednesday when the Lord told me that someone was going to give us a car." During our twenty-eight years of marriage, the Lord had never spoken to either one of us that someone would give us a car. But after He spoke to Cindy, a car was given to us two days later!

The Lord could have given us the car without telling my wife ahead of time, but He spoke to her and our friends to confirm His will and encourage us. God has used our testimony to assure others that He does speak to people today.

Here is another example of how God can speak as we are praying.

Peter Lord, the author of the bestselling book *Hearing God*, was the pastor of Park Avenue Baptist Church in Titusville, Florida, for many years. A number of years ago in December, Peter was praying when God spoke to him.

> I heard God say to me, *I want you to construct a building where people can pray. As proof that this is My idea and not yours, I will send someone to the church that you don't know who will give five hundred dollars toward the building.*
>
> I didn't hear an audible voice, but it came to me as clear words in my mind. I wrote in my prayer journal what the Lord had said.
>
> The next day as I was praying about the chapel, God gave me a deadline: *This will happen before Christmas.* Again I recorded what God had told me, but I didn't tell anyone. . . .

A week passed. No one brought me any money. Two weeks went by, but still no answer. . . . Because time was running out, I started to doubt what I had heard. On December 20, I prayed, "Lord, are you sure you didn't mean by New Year's Day?" . . .

On December 24, a married couple from another city pulled into the church parking lot. They walked into the church and asked to talk to me. . . . I invited the couple into my office, where they introduced themselves.

"Pastor, you don't know us, but when we were praying God spoke to us. He told us to come here and give you some money. We don't really understand why we needed to drive here to give this to you, but we're just being obedient." The couple handed me a check for $500![13]

This was not only confirmation to Peter that he had heard from God, but it also confirmed to the couple that they had also heard Him speak. The prayer chapel was constructed and has been used for many years as a place for people to pray and intercede for others.

2. GOD CAN SPEAK THROUGH DESIRES IN YOUR HEART.

A little boy was flying his kite, which rose into the clouds where it couldn't be seen. A man standing nearby asked him, "How do you know the kite is up there? Maybe it's gone. I can't see it. Can you?"

"No, I can't see it," the boy replied. "But I know it's up there because I can feel a little tug now and then."

The Holy Spirit will lead you by tugging at your heart in the direction you need to go.

Suppose you're looking for employment and must choose between two jobs. Both look like great opportunities, so you pray and ask the Lord which job to take. You understand that He knows the future consequences of both possibilities and He wants to lead you down the best path. So how will you know which job to choose? He will tug at your heart and increase your desire for the correct job.

Of course, this means that we first have to draw near to God and learn what He desires. When you find your joy in pleasing the Lord, you are in a position where He will guide you through your heart. Psalm 37:4 says, "Delight yourself in the LORD and He will give you the desires of your heart." This doesn't mean that everything you want is God's will. It means that when you find your joy in living for God, He places His desires in your heart so you will want what He wants. Once your heart is fully devoted to the Lord, He will lead you without any hindrance or resistance from you.

When I was a new believer, I thought it was selfish to have any desires of my own. I finally realized that I will always have desires as long as I live, but I simply need those desires to be channeled in the right direction.

The Holy Spirit is living inside of every believer in Christ and will act as the "wanter" inside your heart. The prophet Jeremiah warned, "The heart is more deceitful than all else and is desperately sick; who can understand it?" (Jeremiah 17:9). "Following your heart" only works after you have surrendered yourself to do God's will. When you choose to be controlled by the Holy Spirit, He will direct your heart and lead you down the right path.

I've learned to follow the passion in my heart. When you "delight in the LORD" more than anything else, He will place a passion inside your heart and your new desire will be to obey His perfect plan for your life. That's how He leads some people to go overseas to be foreign missionaries, while He tells others to stay where they are right now and faithfully serve Him in their current situation.

> When you find your joy in living for God,
> He places His desires in your heart
> so you will want what He wants.

3. GOD CAN SPEAK THROUGH AN "INNER KNOWING" IN YOUR HEART.

A third way the Lord can speak to you is an "inner knowing" that is similar to having an intuition or a gut feeling. One person described it as, "You know that you know that you know."

During the earliest days of Christianity, the apostles and elders gathered together for the council at Jerusalem to determine the church's stance on circumcision. After much debate, they finally came to a decision.

> *It seemed good* to the apostles and the elders, with the whole church, to choose men from among them to send to Antioch. . . . *It seemed good* to us, having become of one mind, to select men to send to you. . . . For *it seemed good to the Holy Spirit and to us* to lay upon you no greater burden. (Acts 15:22, 25, 28)

These church leaders were praying together to know God's will. Three times the Scripture mentions that "it seemed good" to them. Sometimes God confirms what He is saying by what simply seems right. You can sense in your spirit it's the right thing to do. This assurance comes from the Holy Spirit bearing witness with your spirit. Again, just because something seems good to you doesn't always mean that God is saying yes. The elders prayed through their decision and sought the Lord, and so should you.

The Lord wants to talk with you and guide you through this life. So keep your heart in tune with Him and you will be surprised at what He will reveal to you.

14 | WHY PRAYERS AREN'T ANSWERED LIKE YOU ASKED

"We do not know how to pray as
we should." (Romans 8:26)

Sometimes we pray for our will to be done instead of God's. Jesus taught us the Lord's Prayer but we really don't want to pray it as it's written. We want forgiveness, but don't want to forgive our enemies. We really don't want to be led away from temptation. And so we edit the Lord's Prayer, changing the parts we don't like.

THE LORD'S PRAYER, RSV (REVISED SEVERAL VERSES)

Our Father who art in heaven, hallowed be Thy name.
Thy kingdom come. Thy will be done, on earth as it is in heaven.*
Give us this day our daily bread.**
And forgive us our debts . . .***
And do not lead us into temptation,****
but deliver us from evil.*****
For Thine is the kingdom, and the power, and the glory, forever.
Amen.

* Except when I'm the one who has to do it.
** Forget the bread. Send cash.
*** Deleted from original prayer: "as we also have forgiven
    our debtors."
**** Except when we *want* to be tempted.
***** Only the scary kind of evil.

It's possible to sincerely pray for something that's completely contrary to God's plan. The late Dr. Michael Guido had an evangelistic ministry for many years. When he was attending Moody Bible Institute, a female student asked him to pray for an unspoken prayer request she had. For several weeks he prayed for her, until someone gave him more details about her mysterious request. The girl had a secret crush on Michael and her unspoken request was for them to get married!

He had been praying every day for God to grant her request, even though he didn't know what he was praying for. After discovering her motive, he prayed, "Lord, cancel all my prayers for her." Michael married someone else and they joyfully served the Lord together in ministry their entire lives.

Even two of Jesus' closest disciples didn't understand how to pray correctly. James and John, the two sons of Zebedee, came up to Him, saying, "Teacher, we want You to do for us whatever we ask of You" (Mark 10:35).

Most of us pray that way, don't we? We want to tell Jesus exactly what He needs to do. Ask not what you can do for your God, but what your God can do for you. Rather than rebuking His disciples for being so presumptuous, Jesus asked, "What do you want Me to do for you?" (That didn't necessarily mean He was going to give them their request. There's a huge theological difference between telling Jesus what to do, and Jesus asking us what we want Him to do.)

James and John could have asked for wisdom the way Solomon did when God asked him that same question. Instead, they asked for the top two positions in His kingdom: "Grant that we may sit in Your glory, one on Your right, and one on Your left" (Mark 10:37).

Jesus answered them, "You do not know what you are asking for."

God answers our prayers in one of four ways: "yes," "no," "wait," and "you do not know what you are asking for." The answer to their request was found behind door number four.

> God answers our prayers in one of four ways: yes, no, wait, and "you do not know what you are asking for."

James and John didn't have a clue about what they were asking for. Likewise, most of us don't know what we are asking for either when we pray. We don't always understand the ramifications of what we request from God. Jesus cautioned them that such elite positions come at a costly price. Instead of a throne of glory, He offered them a cup of suffering. "Are you able to drink the cup that I drink?" (v. 38).

Jesus did indeed drink the cup of suffering, being crucified with a thief on His right and another thief on His left. James and John didn't ask to die on crosses with Him, but to sit on thrones with Him. They wanted exaltation, not crucifixion. They didn't understand the costly sacrifice that was required for their request.

We've all had times when we asked God to give us something—but we had no idea what we were asking for, or how it would affect us. When the Lord sent the answer to our prayer, it didn't at all resemble our original idea of what we wanted from Him. And we ask ourselves why.

THE HOLY SPIRIT HELPS US PRAY

God exists in three persons—Father, Son, and Holy Spirit (Matthew 28:19). Jesus told us to pray to the Father in the name of the Son, and the Holy Spirit intercedes for us according to the will of God (Romans 8:26–27). The apostle Paul reveals a valuable insight concerning how prayer works:

> The Spirit also helps our weakness; for *we do not know how to pray as we should*, but the Spirit Himself intercedes for us with groanings too deep for words; and He who searches the hearts knows what the mind of the Spirit is, because He intercedes for the saints according to the will of God. (Romans 8:26–27)

Paul says, "We do not know how to pray as we should." We would be in big trouble if God answered every prayer exactly as we asked. But then he adds some new information—the Holy Spirit helps our weakness.

What's wrong with our prayers? We're ignorant about how to ask rightly. The Spirit reinterprets our human prayers and straightens them out according to God's will. The Holy Spirit helps us by inter-ceding to the Father on our behalf.

The office copier at John McGarvey's church wasn't working, so he called the repair shop. He was unsure how to describe on the phone what was specifically wrong with the copier or which part had broken. The repair shop sent out a technician to take a look at it.

While working on the machine, the repairman called the shop and described the problem and the parts needed to fix it. He used terms that John didn't understand, but technician knew exactly what to say to fix the copier.

John called for help using vague words, but the repairman in-terceded for him to explain what was needed to resolve the issue. This is an illustration of how the Holy Spirit intercedes for us. We call out to the Father in prayer, not knowing exactly what to say, but the Holy Spirit tells Him exactly what we need.[14]

So it only makes sense that when the Father answers our prayers, He's actually answering the intercessions of the Spirit. Otherwise, His intercession of our prayers would be meaningless. That's why *the answer to our prayers might arrive in a different way than we expected*. However, it will be the correct answer and will be the best for us. Isn't that what we really want? Here are four reasons the answers to our prayers might not come exactly as we asked.

> It only makes sense that when the Father answers our prayers, He's actually answering the intercessions of the Spirit.

REASON 1. GOD IS MORE INTERESTED IN SHAPING YOUR CHARACTER THAN GUARANTEEING YOUR COMFORT.

When my daughter was five years old, she came to me crying. "Daddy, I've got a sticker in my finger and I want you to pull it out."

I grabbed some tweezers and held her finger as I attempted minor surgery. At that moment she pulled her hand back and said, "I've changed my mind. I want you to leave it in!"

We all want to stay as comfortable as possible. This isn't necessarily wrong, and sometimes the Lord will deliver us from the problem that afflicts us. But at other times He won't answer the way we asked, because He's more interested in developing patience, dependency on Him, and other qualities within us.

The apostle Paul was tormented by a "thorn in the flesh" and asked God three times to get His heavenly tweezers and remove it. That sticker produced a great deal of suffering, which Paul described as a "messenger of Satan to torment me" (2 Corinthians 12:7). He probably believed that this satanic messenger couldn't possibly be permitted by God and assumed he would receive immediate relief from it. But after he had called for help three times, Paul had to be wondering if the Lord had heard his request. God did hear his prayers, but answered differently than Paul had asked:

> Because of the surpassing greatness of the revelations, for this reason, to keep me from exalting myself, there was given me a thorn in the flesh, a messenger of Satan to torment me—to keep me from exalting myself! Concerning this I implored the Lord three times that it might leave me. And He has said to me, "My grace is sufficient for you, for power is perfected in weakness." Most gladly, therefore, I will rather boast about my weaknesses, so that the power of Christ may dwell in me. (2 Corinthians 12:7–9)

God did answer his prayer. It just wasn't in the way he had asked. The Lord didn't take away his thorn but gave him the grace to endure it instead. He explained to Paul that this thorn served a purpose that would be for his benefit. If Paul hadn't learned to hear God speak to him, he never would have understood why the Lord answered differently than he had asked.

If Paul hadn't learned to hear God speak to him, he never would have understood why the Lord answered differently than he had asked.

Paul had received so many incredible divine revelations and insights that he could have easily become proud and thought he had received "Most Favored by God" status over everyone else. The thorn in his flesh was a messenger of Satan. The Greek word for "messenger" also means "angel." It was a fallen angel, or demon, who incited tremendous persecution against him (see 2 Corinthians 11:23–27). The Lord would use Paul's suffering through others' hate and rejection to keep him from exalting himself. Paul had to stay humble so God's power could continue to flow through him to help others in need.

REASON 2. GOD HAS SOMETHING BETTER FOR YOU THAN WHAT YOU ARE PRAYING FOR.

We usually think we know precisely what we need, but God always knows what's best for us. Since He knows the future and can see the outcome of every possible decision, He will sometimes deny what we ask for because it would prevent something better that He has planned for us.

Years ago, my friend's fiancée broke off their engagement, which was the most painful event of his life. He plunged into deep depression and didn't think he would ever pull out of it. He prayed that she would have a change of heart and they would get back together. At the time, he didn't realize God had allowed the breakup because He had someone else in mind for him.

My friend said, "Three months after my fiancée cancelled our wedding, I met another woman and completely forgot about my old girlfriend. I knew she was the one for me. We've now been happily married over thirty years. God knew I had to be rejected by my first fiancée so I could be available to meet my true soulmate from Him. Now whenever I think about my fiancée rejecting me, I smile and thank God that we didn't get married!"

The Lord often doesn't answer our prayers like we want Him to because He has something much better planned. Andrew Murray said, "God reserves the very best for those who leave the choice with

Him." As we wait for Him to provide, we must continue to trust Him and remember His promise: "No good thing does He withhold from those who walk uprightly" (Psalm 84:11).

REASON 3. GOD WANTS TO ANSWER YOUR PRAYER IN A TOTALLY DIFFERENT WAY THAN YOU EXPECTED.

King Herod put the apostle James to death with the sword. This was the same James whom Jesus had asked, "Are you able to drink the cup that I drink?" (Matthew 10:38). Then Herod arrested Peter and was apparently planning to kill him as well.

"So Peter was kept in the prison, but prayer for him was being made fervently by the church to God" (Acts 12:5). Although we don't know what they were praying, they probably said, "Lord, soften Herod's heart and change his mind. Lord, send someone with a set of keys to let Peter out. Lord, save the guards and have them free him." Although they prayed for his release, they were caught off guard by how God actually accomplished it. Here's how He answered their prayers:

> On the very night when Herod was about to bring him forward, Peter was sleeping between two soldiers, bound with two chains, and guards in front of the door were watching over the prison. And behold, *an angel of the Lord suddenly appeared* and *a light shone in the cell*; and he struck Peter's side and woke him up, saying, "Get up quickly." And *his chains fell off* his hands. And the angel said to him, "Gird yourself and put on your sandals." And he did so. And he said to him, "Wrap your cloak around you and follow me." And he went out and continued to follow, and he did not know that what was being done by the angel was real, but thought he was seeing a vision. When they had passed the first and second guard, *they came to the iron gate* that leads into the city, *which opened for them by itself*; and they went out and went along one street, and immediately the angel departed from him. (Acts 12:6–10, italics mine)

An angel appeared and woke him up, a light shone in the cell, Peter's chains fell off his hands, the angel led him out of jail, and the iron gate opened by itself. This was the second time an angel sprung him out of prison (Acts 5:19). We aren't told why the soldiers didn't do anything to stop the escape, although God probably made sure they slept through the getaway.

Peter immediately went to the house of Mary, the mother of Mark, where many people were gathered together praying for his release:

> When he knocked at the door of the gate, a servant-girl named Rhoda came to answer. When she recognized Peter's voice, because of her joy she did not open the gate, but ran in and announced that Peter was standing in front of the gate. *They said to her, "You are out of your mind!"* But she kept insisting that it was so. They kept saying, "It is his angel." But Peter continued knocking; and when they had opened the door, they saw him and were amazed. (Acts 12:13–16)

Perhaps they didn't believe that Peter was already out of jail, because God had answered them quite differently than they had asked. They weren't expecting their prayers to be answered that quickly, and they certainly couldn't fathom the extraordinary way the Lord released Peter from his chains and imprisonment.

The lesson? Quit trying to figure out how God will answer your prayer. It will probably happen in a way that you aren't expecting.

REASON 4. GOD WILL SOMETIMES DENY YOUR REQUEST TO PROTECT YOU FROM HARM.

If I am praying for something and God keeps saying no, then He must know something that I don't. Since He knows every possible outcome of what I'm praying for, I've learned to let Him determine how the answer comes. He loves me so much that if I ask for something that will harm me, He will deny my request and withhold it for my good. He's trying to protect me, not punish me.

Sometimes the reason God denied your request will become obvious later. But you may never know in this life why the Lord did not come through with the answer you wanted so badly. He never promised to explain every situation or answer every question that puzzles us. "The secret things belong to the LORD our God, but the things revealed belong to us and to our sons forever" (Deuteronomy 29:29). The "secret things" are those mysteries that aren't going to be explained during our lifetime.

If I am praying for something and God keeps saying no, then He must know something that I don't.

When you get to heaven and stand face to face with Jesus, your knowledge will be expanded and every question you have ever had will be answered (1 Corinthians 13:12). Until then, place your trust in the God who does understand everything.

The next time your prayers aren't answered as you had hoped, remember that it's probably for one of these four reasons, and it's for your good in the grand scheme of things.

PART 2

ANSWERS TO QUESTIONS

15 | IF I PRAY FOR WISDOM, HOW DO I KNOW WHEN I GET IT?

"For the LORD gives wisdom;
From His mouth come knowledge and
understanding." (Proverbs 2:6)

There's a joke about a group of people praying together. Suddenly, an angel appears and says to one man, "I'll give you a choice. You can have money, long life, or wisdom. Which do you want?"

Without hesitation he says, "I'll take wisdom."

The angel says, "Done. You now have the ability to make wise decisions," and disappears.

Everyone looks at the man, who has a shocked look on his face. Finally someone says, "Now that you can make wise decisions, tell us what you're thinking."

The man sighs and says, "I should have taken the money."

Solomon found himself in a similar situation, but this was no joke. The Lord appeared to him in a dream and said, "Ask what you wish me to give you" (1 Kings 3:5). Solomon could have chosen money, a yacht, or a huge mansion. Instead, he asked for the wisdom to lead Israel as their king. "It was pleasing in the sight of the LORD that Solomon had asked this thing" (1 Kings 3:9). As a bonus, God decided to give him the extra benefits of riches, honor, and long life.

Since Solomon now had wisdom from God, he knew how to handle those extra blessings correctly. After all, what good is a long life if you're miserable because you make terrible decisions? How can more money help you if you lose it through overspending and bad investments? What benefit is it to be king but not know how to lead a nation down the right path? Acquiring God's wisdom can change your destiny, which can produce a better life for you.

The Scripture says, "If anyone lacks wisdom let him ask of God" (James 1:5). Is there anyone who *doesn't* need wisdom? Whenever we're confused, God always knows what to do and is willing to tell us. If you bring your problem to the Lord, He will never say, "Wow, that's a tough one. I never thought about that before. I'm sorry, but I don't know what to tell you." He knows everything and always gives the correct advice concerning what to do.

Wisdom is the ability to see your situation as God sees it. Common sense sees the obvious, but wisdom is the ability to see beyond the obvious. Wisdom is knowing how to make right decisions. Think how much it would be worth and how much heartache you would avoid if every decision you made was the right one.

Common sense sees the obvious,
but wisdom is the ability to
see beyond the obvious.

Preparing to Receive Wisdom

Solomon became the wisest man on earth because the Lord "downloaded" His wisdom into him. The same God who showed him what to do can do the same for you. He wants to send His wisdom from His throne to your heart and mind, but you must first be prepared to receive it. Four things are necessary:

1. Humble yourself before God.

A young man asked his pastor if he would teach him God's ways. The pastor picked up a coffee pot and started pouring coffee into the student's cup. The cup filled up and began to overflow. He continued to pour until it was spilling onto the floor.

The young man said, "Hey, quit pouring! The cup is full!"

The pastor replied, "That's your first lesson. If you're full of yourself there's no room for God. It's not possible to learn the ways of God until you first empty yourself."

Solomon humbled himself before the Lord and said, "I am but a little child; I do not know how to go out or come in" (1 Kings 3:7). He called himself a little child, but Solomon was actually about twenty years old when he took the throne. Still, he acknowledged to the Lord that he didn't have the ability to lead the nation of Israel and needed supernatural insight.

If we really want to receive wisdom from above, we must stop trusting in our own human reasoning. Solomon later passed on this advice: "Trust in the LORD with all your heart and do not lean on your own understanding. In all your ways acknowledge Him and He will make your paths straight" (Proverbs 3:5–6).

2. HAVE A TEACHABLE SPIRIT THAT'S WILLING TO RECEIVE INSTRUCTION.

"The fear of the LORD is the beginning of wisdom" (Proverbs 9:10). Wisdom begins by having a reverential fear of God, knowing that He is all-powerful and all-knowing. A teachable spirit means you're willing to follow your advisor's instructions even *before* you hear them because you have complete trust in that person.

Solomon asked for "an understanding heart" (1 Kings 3:9). The Hebrew word literally means "a hearing heart." He wanted to be tuned in to the voice of God. If the greatest teacher in the world has a student who doesn't want to learn, the instructor will be wasting her time. It's impossible to receive God's wisdom without first having a teachable spirit that is willing to obey the advice given.

3. ASK IN FAITH WITHOUT DOUBTING.

"But if any of you lacks wisdom, let him ask of God, who gives to all generously and without reproach, and *it will be given* to him. But he must ask in faith without any doubting" (James 1:5–6). God doesn't automatically share His wisdom with everyone on earth. You must ask for it with faith and expectancy, knowing He will give it to you.

Be specific in your request. What exactly do you need wisdom for? Do you need wisdom to raise your children? Do you need it to make a right decision? Are you dealing with a difficult relationship, or are you unsure how to handle your finances? Solomon specifically requested wisdom to rule a nation. He prayed, "So give Your servant an understanding heart to judge Your people to discern between good and evil. For who is able to judge this great people of Yours?" (1 Kings 3:9). You might not be leading a nation, but you can bring your own situations and responsibilities to God to ask for His guidance.

4. RECEIVE IT AS A GIFT FROM GOD.

"But he must *ask* in faith without any doubting, for the one who doubts . . . ought not to expect that he will *receive* anything from the Lord" (James 1:6–7). Notice the two parts of this verse—we must ask and we must expect to receive. Many people will ask God to show them what to do, but they don't believe that He will actually answer their request.

Your local radio station is sending out signals at this very moment. You don't hear them because you need a radio to pick up the sound waves. The station is constantly broadcasting signals but you need a radio to receive them.

God sends His wisdom signals to all who ask, but we must have a receiver to hear them. The "receiver" who hears God's thoughts is the Holy Spirit, who indwells everyone who loves Christ. "For who among men knows the thoughts of a man except the spirit of the man, which is in him? Even so *the thoughts of God no one knows except the Spirit of God*" (1 Corinthians 2:11).

Just because God gives wisdom doesn't mean everyone will receive it. Have you ever tried to give a gift to someone who doesn't want it? You hold out the gift and the person says, "No, I can't take that. I'm not worthy." We must be willing to receive His divine wisdom as a gift from Him.

Three Ways God Will Grant His Wisdom

When you pray for wisdom, how do you know when it comes to you? It will be obvious because you'll receive divine insight about what to do in your situation. The Lord typically gives wisdom through three avenues—the Bible, thoughts in your mind, and wise people.

1. He will speak to you through the Scriptures.

The Lord speaks wisdom through His written word. When you read the Bible and a verse grabs your heart and a light bulb comes on in your mind, it's usually the Holy Spirit (who inspired the Scripture in the first place) speaking to you. "For the word of God is *living and active and sharper* than any two-edged sword" (Hebrews 4:12). God's Spirit is enlightening you through that passage. It may be that a story in the Bible is similar to the situation you're going through and the Lord is giving your answer through that Scripture passage.

If you aren't seeking the Lord through reading the Scriptures on a regular basis, you will miss the wisdom He wants to give. Jesus said, "The Helper, the Holy Spirit, whom the Father will send in My name, He will teach you all things, and bring to your remembrance all that I said to you" (John 14:26). The Spirit will enlighten the words of Jesus to reveal their meaning to you. He will bring to your mind certain verses that will guide you in how to proceed in your situation.

2. He will put thoughts in your mind about what to do.

We've already discussed in chapter 13, "God Wants to Speak to You," that the Lord can put thoughts into your mind. When you ask God for wisdom and then an idea pops into your mind, don't be too quick to dismiss that thought. It might be the answer to your problem that you just prayed about. The Lord will send His wisdom as thoughts to your mind, which will point you in a particular direction or will give you insight into how to solve your dilemma.

But don't assume that every thought that comes to your mind is God speaking to you. You must discern which ideas are from Him and which are not (see Hebrews 5:14). When the Holy Spirit speaks thoughts to your mind, they will never contradict or disagree with God's written Word. From my own experience, I have found that He will keep bringing the right information back to my mind and reinforcing the correct way to go. The Lord promises us, "I will instruct you and teach you in the way which you should go; I will counsel you with My eye upon you" (Psalm 32:8).

3. HE WILL USE WISE PEOPLE TO ADVISE YOU.

Some people won't listen to anyone's advice because they think they already know the answers to everything. No one can tell them what to do. The Scripture says the one who won't receive instruction is a fool. "The way of a fool is right in his own eyes but a wise man is he who listens to counsel" (Proverbs 12:15). One way the Lord speaks to us is through wise people who have insight into our situation.

But beware of listening to the wrong people. There's no shortage of people who would love to give you the wrong information. People with impure hearts will advise you with ulterior motives; sometimes they want to manipulate you for their own gain, or they might even want to see you destroyed by sending you down the wrong path. God's Word tells us, "How blessed is the man who does not walk in the counsel of the wicked" (Psalm 1:1). Don't listen to just everyone's advice, but carefully select counselors who know Jesus and live out their faith. The Lord will speak to you through believers who have been walking with Him.

Ask advice from those who have a track record of making wise decisions. Again, Solomon wrote: "For *by wise guidance* you will wage war and in abundance of counselors there is victory" (Proverbs 24:6). If you're going into a battle, never follow the advice of those who are inexperienced in warfare. Don't engage in combat based on the instruction of someone who has never had to dodge bullets or doesn't understand military tactics.

And don't listen to those who cannot get their own lives together. Never ask a drowning person to show you how to swim. If it doesn't work for them, it won't work for you. You might be tempted to listen to those who have the same problems as yours. They might make you feel good through their sympathy because they know what you are going through. But they can't solve your problem because they don't know how to fix their own.

> Never ask a drowning person
> to show you how to swim.

Applying Wisdom

"So teach us to number our days, that we may apply our hearts unto wisdom" (Psalm 90:12 KJV). All the wisdom in the world won't do any good if you don't apply the advice to your life's struggles. Solomon used his wisdom to solve problems and lead a nation. You must also apply the Lord's wisdom to the problems you face every day at your job, at school, in your relationships, and in handling your finances.

We will all face many problems during our lifetimes, but with the wisdom of God we can solve every one of them.

PRAYER

Heavenly Father, I humble myself before you. I don't know what to do in this situation but I know you do and you've promised to guide me. I ask you to give me wisdom and show me what to do about (*name the situation*). I believe that you will give your wisdom to me and I receive it now in Jesus' name. I will apply what you reveal to me to my current situation and I will trust you with the outcome. In Jesus' name.

16 | WHY DOES GOD WANT ME TO PRAY FOR MY ENEMIES?

"Pray for those who mistreat you." (Luke 6:28)

Praying for those who mistreat us is the last thing we feel like doing. It goes against our nature to pray for them. Not only do we not want to do it, we're ready for God to punish them!

But since Jesus is the one who answers our prayers, He must have told us to do this for a good reason. He wouldn't have commanded us to pray for those who mistreat us if it didn't make any difference. He has several reasons, but here's one that will motivate you—praying for your enemies is the key to releasing God's blessing on your life.

In the Old Testament, Satan attacked a righteous man named Job and took away his children, property, and health. To make matters worse, three of Job's friends turned against him and falsely accused him of causing his own misfortune through hidden sin in his life. This wasn't true, since the Lord had said this about Job: "There is no one like him on the earth, a blameless and upright man, fearing God and turning away from evil" (Job 1:8). Perhaps you can identify with Job if you've ever been gossiped about or slandered when you hadn't done anything wrong.

The turning point in Job's trial came when he chose to pray for those who wrongly accused him. The Scripture tells us, "The LORD restored the fortunes of Job *when he prayed for his friends*, and the LORD increased all that Job had twofold" (Job 42:10). But what if he hadn't prayed for them? Perhaps God would have withheld His blessings.

How Are We Supposed to Pray for Our Enemies?

Jesus said, "Bless those who curse you. Pray for those who mistreat you" (Luke 6:28). He also said, "Love your enemies and pray for those who persecute you" (Matthew 5:44). He commanded us to pray for them—but He never told us exactly *what* we are to pray. Could we be praying for the wrong thing? Are we to pray for our enemies to be punished, to be blessed, or something else?

Should we ask God to punish them? Although this is the first thing we would usually like the Lord to do, asking for instant justice might be jumping the gun. Yes, people who hurt others will ultimately be punished if they don't change their hearts and surrender to God. But even though they might deserve it (just the way we do), God doesn't want anyone, including the people who have hurt us, to be punished by being completely cut off from Him. He wants us to pray for them with a higher purpose—to bring them to repentance so they will get right with Him. When a person has a genuine change of heart, their critical attitudes and destructive behavior will stop, which is what the Lord desires.

When you are tempted to ask God to punish someone else for the way they've hurt you, take a second to examine yourself. Are there any people whom *you* have hurt, offended, or cursed? Instead of asking the Lord to punish others, thank Him for the way He has forgiven you of your own sins and brought you back to Him in repentance. Otherwise, you'll be like the unforgiving slave who was pardoned by his master but couldn't forgive his fellow slave (Matthew 18:23–35).

Are we supposed to pray for God to bless them? Some people assume that Jesus' words mean we are supposed to pray for the Lord's blessing on our enemies. Really? Even if they are proud and rebellious? What about the verse that says, "For rebellion is as the sin of witchcraft" (1 Samuel 15:23)? And what about the Scripture that says "God is opposed to the proud but gives grace to the humble" (1 Peter 5:5)? If I am proud and rebellious, I shouldn't pray for the Lord to bless me, so why would I ask Him to bless an arrogant, rebellious person who continually mistreats others?

When Jesus said "bless those who curse you," He didn't mean to pray for God to send His blessings on your enemy. Cursing means someone is spewing out evil words to you, but blessing means saying good words to someone. Jesus said that when evil people curse us, we should reply by speaking to them kindly.

Instead of praying for God to either punish our enemies, or to bless them no matter how evil they may behave, we have a third option—to pray they will have a change of heart. God's will is "for all to come to repentance" (2 Peter 3:9). The only way people can have a lasting change of heart is if the Holy Spirit convicts them of their wrongdoing. Praying for those who mistreat you is the beginning of the process of repentance. We should still want our enemies to be blessed in the long run—after all, this is what Christ wanted for *us* when we were still sinners and enemies of God (Romans 5:8, 10). But it is certainly right to recognize that the people who have hurt us need to get right with God before we can ask Him to bless them in other ways.

> The only way people can have a lasting change of heart is if the Holy Spirit convicts them of their wrongdoing.

God wants to change the sinful hearts of those who treat you harshly. When they truly repent and get right with the Lord, they will then be motivated to change the way they behave toward you and others.

Zacchaeus, who was a corrupt tax collector, is an example of a hardened man whose life was changed by Jesus. The Roman government hired people who lived in Israel to collect their taxes for them. Tax collecting was a lucrative job that was auctioned off to the highest bidder. Only dishonest people wanted the job because they could overcharge people and pocket the difference. Jews viewed tax-gatherers (also called publicans) as legalized thieves and traitors who were more loyal to their foreign oppressor, Rome, than to Israel.

The Pharisees believed tax collectors were the most evil reprobates on the planet, so they separated them into a category even lower than sinners—which explains why the Bible speaks of "tax collectors and sinners" (See Matthew 9:10–11, 11:19). According to the Pharisees, tax collectors could never receive eternal life. They taught that whenever a tax collector died, heaven rejoiced as he was being dropped into hell.[15] Jesus took their words and corrected them, saying there's rejoicing in heaven when a sinner repents—not when someone goes to hell (Luke 15:7, 10).

When a person became a tax collector, he did it with the understanding that God detested him so much that he had no hope of ever making it to heaven. Zacchaeus was a chief tax gatherer, meaning he had worked his way up to a higher position. He was rich and probably gained his wealth by defrauding countless people out of their money over the years.

Now you understand Zacchaeus's spiritual condition and state of mind on the day Jesus came to town. His only friends were fellow tax collectors. He had assumed it was impossible for him to ever be accepted by God. Because he was a small man, he had to climb up a tree to see over the crowd to get a glimpse of Jesus.

As Jesus was passing by that tree, He looked up and called him by name: "Zacchaeus, hurry and come down, for today I must stay at your house" (Luke 19:5). Although Jesus had never met him before, He knew his name. And He knows your name too.

Jesus put His reputation on the line. If He stayed at Zacchaeus's house, people would assume He had placed His stamp of approval on the stealing and fraud done by tax gatherers. His request to stay at this publican's house must have made the Pharisees furious. Never mind the fact that Jesus had told them, "Truly I say to you that the tax collectors and prostitutes will get into the kingdom of God before you" (Matthew 21:30). He explained that the tax gatherers and prostitutes had repented of their sins as a result of John the Baptist's preaching, but the self-righteous Pharisees hadn't.

Zacchaeus could have been a stingy, greedy swindler—like Ebenezer Scrooge and Bernie Madoff wrapped up into one person.

But after he had a personal encounter with Jesus, he became convicted of his sins and realized how horribly he had mistreated others. He told Jesus, "Behold, Lord, half of my possessions I will give to the poor, and if I have defrauded anyone of anything, I will give back four times as much" (Luke 19:8).

Jesus didn't need tell him to do this. He knew that his transformed heart would bring about a change in his behavior. Zacchaeus was so convinced of his wrongdoing that he not only decided to stop overcharging people, but he also made a commitment to quadruple his repayment to everyone he had defrauded.

It would take him an enormous amount of time to meticulously look through his records to find all the people he had cheated—and then go to their houses to generously pay them restitution. God miraculously transformed him from a pilferer to a philanthropist.

Do you think that your enemies are too set in their ways to be redeemed or that it would do no good to pray for them? Zacchaeus proves that anyone, no matter how corrupt they are, can experience a change of heart. Jesus taught, "with God all things are possible" (Matthew 19:26).

Zacchaeus would never have changed if he hadn't met Jesus. But when he humbled himself before the Lord, he immediately wanted to make restitution with everyone. We typically want others to sincerely apologize to us and make things right, but we ignore their need to get right with God first. It doesn't work that way. After your enemies get right with God, they will get right with you.

If a dishonest man like Zacchaeus can experience such a radical change of heart, then it's possible for your enemies' hearts to break in repentance—and this is the reason you must pray for them. So don't stop interceding for them until they humbly bow before the Lord. You'll know that they have sincerely turned to God, because their actions will tell the story.

> After your enemies get right with
> God, they will get right with you.

THREE REASONS TO PRAY FOR THOSE WHO MISTREAT YOU

REASON 1. PRAYING FOR YOUR ENEMIES PROTECTS YOUR HEART FROM RESENTMENT.

When we are mistreated and abused by someone, we must be on guard so that seeds of anger and resentment aren't planted in the soil of our hearts. Jesus told us to pray for our enemies for a reason. As we intercede for those who have hurt us, it keeps us from dwelling on the way they mistreated us.

We cannot effectively pray for our enemies if we are angry at them. Forgiveness does not mean that we excuse what they did, or admit that their abuse wasn't wrong. Nor does it mean, if they committed a crime, that they should be exempt from punishment or going to jail. Prison might be the very place they need to be to keep them from committing more crimes. Forgiveness simply means that you release the anger out of your heart and leave their mistreatment of you in God's hands.

When Jesus was crucified, He could have called twelve legions of angels to come to His defense (Matthew 26:53). With a simple word from Him, the sky could have been filled with a host of mighty angels that could have annihilated every one of His enemies. Jesus never called for this heavenly force to execute judgment, because He wanted His executors' hearts to change. He prayed, "Father, forgive them; *for they do not know what they are doing*" (Luke 23:34).

How could the men crucifying Him not know what they were doing? They didn't grasp the terrible judgment they would face for their mistreatment of God's Son if they didn't repent. The apostle Paul said that none of rulers at that time understood what they were doing, "for if they had understood it, they would not have crucified the Lord of glory" (1 Corinthians 2:8). But their ignorance wasn't the end of the story. Jesus's sacrifice made it possible for sinners to be set free from the terrifying eternal consequences of their sin. Praying for your enemies draws you right back to Christ's sacrifice on the cross, the source of all freedom and forgiveness.

Perhaps you are struggling to forgive someone. You might say you just can't do it, but you *can* forgive when God gives you the grace to do it. His grace gives you the supernatural ability to forgive and to do things that you cannot do in your own human strength. When you are struggling to forgive, always remember that Jesus not only died for your sins, but also for the sins your enemy has committed against you.

REASON 2. PRAYING FOR YOUR ENEMIES HELPS TO BRING THEM TO REPENTANCE.

Sometimes it looks as though our enemies are getting away with their evil behavior without suffering any consequences. In fact, they might even look like they're blessed and not in trouble with God at all. The psalmist Asaph said, "These are the wicked; and always at ease, they have increased in wealth. . . . When I pondered to understand this, it was troublesome in my sight until I came into the sanctuary of God; then I perceived their end" (Psalm 73:12, 16–17). Evil people are headed toward eternal judgment unless they repent. We should never forget that the Bible warns, "It is a terrifying thing to fall into the hands of the hands of the living God" (Hebrews 10:31).

For a long time I had no idea what I was supposed to pray for those who mistreated me, but as I was studying the book of Jonah the answer became clear.

God sent the prophet Jonah to preach a message of judgment to the people of Nineveh: "Forty days and Nineveh will be overthrown" (Jonah 3:4). If anyone deserved God's judgment, it was the Ninevites. They were an extremely cruel people. When they conquered their enemies in battle, they would maim them by cutting off their hands, ears, noses, and tongues, or gouging out their eyes.

Jonah marched up and down the streets of Nineveh preaching God's judgment for their wickedness. When the king and the entire city heard of the destruction God had planned for them, they humbled themselves and turned from their evil ways. After they bowed their hearts in repentance, the Lord halted His plan to destroy them.

You'd think Jonah would have been thrilled about the Ninevites turning to the Lord, but not so with this angry prophet. Instead, he was furious because he thought their atrocities shouldn't be forgiven so quickly. Jonah desperately wanted God to destroy them without granting them even an ounce of mercy.

After they changed their hearts and their ways, the Lord asked Jonah, "Should I not have compassion on Nineveh, the great city?" (Jonah 4:11). Since God showed them mercy, He wanted Jonah to have mercy on them too.

The lesson is clear. The Lord wants us to have mercy on the cruel people who mistreat us; He wants us to pray that they will humble themselves before Him and change their ways. After they surrender their lives and turn from their evil ways, He will bless and show compassion to them. The Lord prefers to bless your enemies after they have truly repented of their sins rather than punish them.

REASON 3. PRAYING FOR YOUR ENEMIES RELEASES THE HOLY SPIRIT TO CONVICT THEM OF THEIR ABUSIVE BEHAVIOR.

As we have already discussed, the second purpose of prayer is for us to be participants in accomplishing God's will on earth. When an innocent person prays for a guilty person, it touches the Lord's heart and moves Him to action.

In the book of Acts, Stephen hadn't done anything wrong when he was murdered by his persecutors. All he had done was preach a message about Jewish history. The congregation didn't like his sermon that day so they picked up rocks and cast their votes. As he was being stoned, Stephen cried out to God, "Lord, do not hold this sin against them!" (Acts 7:60).

He was going to die within a matter of seconds. In the blink of an eye, he would be standing face to face with God Almighty. He didn't want to enter heaven and face his Creator with unforgiveness in his heart. So as his persecutors stoned him, he prayed for the Lord to forgive them. No matter how hateful they were to him, it didn't stop Stephen from praying for their salvation.

A young man named Saul watched Stephen being stoned and gave his hearty approval. His fellow Pharisees laid their garments at Saul's feet and he was "watching out for the coats of those who were slaying him" (Acts 22:20). Saul thought protecting their coats from being stolen was more important than protecting an innocent man from being murdered. He must have believed keeping the eighth commandment was more important than keeping the sixth.

When a person is spiritually blind, they can't see what's very obvious to others. When we pray for those who mistreat us, we ask God to open their spiritual eyes so they will realize how they have devastated others. We must pray that the Holy Spirit will convict them of their sins so they will repent and escape God's judgment.

Saul made it his mission to persecute and imprison those who followed Jesus. One day as he traveled toward Damascus, a light from heaven blinded him and he was converted to be a disciple of Christ. Saul later became an apostle and wrote much of the New Testament.

Could there be a link between Stephen's prayer for his persecutors just before he died and this coat-watcher's conversion on the road to Damascus? Why would the Bible mention that Saul was present when Stephen was stoned if there wasn't a connection between the two? I believe these two events are indeed linked, and God revealed himself to Saul in response to Stephen's dying prayer for him.

When an innocent person prays for his or her persecutors, God will intervene and bring conviction on those who oppress others. Something happens in the spiritual realm when we forgive and pray for our enemies. Jesus said, "Whatever you bind on earth shall be bound in heaven; and whatever you loose on earth shall have been loosed in heaven" (Matthew 18:18).

Here we see a connection between the natural realm and the spiritual realm. When we forgive and let go of those who have hurt us and begin to intercede for them, the Holy Spirit is "released" to reveal to them how their sins and abusive behavior have been injuring others.

Only the Holy Spirit can bring conviction of sin. Jesus told His disciples, "And He [the Holy Spirit], when He comes, will convict the world concerning sin and righteousness and judgment" (John 16:8). God desires for your enemy to change and the process begins *when the victim prays for the one who caused the hurt.* The grace of God can reach the most hardened heart when forgiveness is unconditionally offered to those who have hurt us the most.

> The grace of God can reach the most hardened heart when forgiveness is unconditionally offered to those who have hurt us the most.

WATCH YOUR ATTITUDE WHEN GOD BEGINS TO PUT PRESSURE ON YOUR ENEMY.

God may bring punishment to your enemy in this life. It's certainly right to pray that the police will arrest the criminal who harmed you. But even if the offender isn't brought to justice in prison, the Lord has ways to make your enemy extremely miserable as part of the process of bringing him or her to repentance.

If you see your enemy's world starting to fall apart, be careful not to gloat or be happy about it. Don't let it give you the slightest bit of pleasure. You certainly wouldn't be happy if the people you love were crushed in this way, and Jesus tells us to "love our enemies" just the way He did.

Your improper response could even interfere with God's plan to humble the person who hurt you. "Do not rejoice when your enemy falls, and do not let your heart be glad when he stumbles, or the LORD will see it and be displeased, and turn His anger away from him" (Proverbs 24:17–18). This passage states that God is watching both you and your enemy. If you are thrilled when you see your enemy being punished, He will remove His hand from the situation.

Keep in mind that the primary reason you're praying is to bring your enemy to repentance. The answer to your prayer will be obvious when the person is genuinely sorry for what he or she did, and when he or she gets right with both God and you. You don't want to do anything that will stop this.

But suppose your enemy doesn't repent. What if the person never apologizes? What if the individual never changes? God tells us that we must not take our own revenge, because vengeance is His right alone. "Never take your own revenge, beloved, but leave room for the wrath of God, for it is written, 'VENGEANCE IS MINE, I WILL REPAY,' says the Lord" (Romans 12:19).

He will make sure that justice will prevail. The people who mistreated you will either repent of their hateful actions, or they will be punished by God. But remember that the Lord desires their repentance foremost and vengeance is always His last resort. Your prayers for your enemies play an important part in them humbling themselves and getting right with Him—and with you.

PRAYER

Lord, because you have graciously forgiven all my sins, and because you died for the sins that people have committed against me, I choose to forgive (*name the person*). I choose to let go of my hurt. I pray you will convict (*name*) of (*his/her*) rebellious attitude, that (*he/she*) will repent and get right with you, and will apologize for the hurt (*he/she*) did to me. I know you will be pleased if my enemy has a change of heart, and after (*he/she*) does, I ask you to bless (*him/her*).

17 | IF MORE PEOPLE PRAY IS IT MORE LIKELY TO BE ANSWERED?

> "The prayer of a righteous person is
> powerful and effective." (James 5:16 NIV)

We've all received emails or seen social media posts asking us to pray for an urgent need of someone we don't know. We assume that if more people pray it will increase the chances of the request being answered by God. But is that true? The answer to this question can be found by examining what moves God's heart to respond to prayer requests. James tells us:

> The effective, fervent prayer of a righteous man avails much. Elijah was a man with a nature like ours, and he prayed earnestly that it would not rain; and it did not rain on the land for three years and six months. And he prayed again, and the heaven gave rain, and the earth produced its fruit. (James 5:16–18)

Elijah was the only person praying, yet his prayer was so effective that it stopped raining in Israel for over three years. At the end of that time, he prayed again and the rain poured. Two clues in this passage reveal what makes prayer effective.

1. THE PRAYER IS OFFERED BY A RIGHTEOUS PERSON.

First, notice that the prayer is offered by a person who loves God. The Lord knows the praying person's integrity and personal walk with Him. The Scripture tells us that "The LORD is far from the wicked, but He hears the prayer of the righteous" (Proverbs 15:29). When an individual with a pure heart makes a special request, God typically responds by answering his or her prayer.

When God was ready to destroy Sodom, Abraham asked the Lord if He would spare them from destruction if fifty righteous people lived in the city. The Lord said, "If I find in Sodom fifty righteous within the city, then I will spare the whole place on their account" (Genesis 18:26). Abraham kept lowering the number until he finally got to ten. The Lord promised that He wouldn't destroy Sodom if only ten righteous people lived in the city. Tragically, not even ten righteous people could be found.

God's heart is moved to act on behalf of righteous people. He sees the integrity and purity of our hearts when we approach Him with our request.

2. THE PRAYER IS EFFECTIVE BECAUSE IT'S PASSIONATE.

The prayer is described as "effective" and "fervent," which means that it's prayed with passion and energy. God loves when we pray with fiery purpose and zeal. He's not impressed by ritualistic prayers or mumbling a few sentences just to say we've prayed. If we're not serious about what we're praying for, then why should He take our request seriously?

An urgent request will typically motivate more people to pray than if people think the request isn't that important. Because people are often consumed with praying for their own needs, their hearts must be stirred to pray for someone else's need.

So then, if more people pray for the same request, is it more likely to be answered? The answer is yes, if godly people are passionately praying for the same particular request. Paul told the Corinthian church, "You also joining in helping us through your prayers, so that thanks may be given by many persons on our behalf for the favor bestowed on us *through the prayers of many*" (2 Corinthians 1:11). He was acknowledging all the good things that had already come from "the prayers of many" and was asking the Corinthians to join with him and all the churches in praising God.

When righteous people pray in agreement with a sense of urgency, it increases the likelihood of a miracle taking place. Jesus told His disciples, "Again I say to you, that if two of you agree on earth about anything that they may ask, it shall be done for them by My Father who is in heaven" (Matthew 18:19). He said that just two people can bring the answer, if they pray in agreement. It's even better if two hundred pray in unity.

> When righteous people pray in agreement with a sense of urgency, it increases the likelihood of a miracle taking place.

But that doesn't mean that God will only hear your request if it has a thousand "likes" on Facebook. Don't confuse godliness and passionate urgency with popularity. Remember Elijah? He was just one man "with a nature like ours," yet his prayer moved God to miraculously withhold rain for more than three years. Many people praying together will reach God's heart, not necessarily because of their numbers, but because they are all passionate about seeing His will done on the earth. If you're praying for something and no one else cares to pray with you, don't give up. The causes that are closest to God's heart aren't always the ones that are popular with the rest of the world.

However, when a nation is in rebellion and heading for judgment, it will probably require most of God's people in the nation to humble themselves and seek His face for Him to stop His plans. The Lord told King Solomon:

> "If I shut up the heavens so that there is no rain, or if I command the locust to devour the land, or if I send pestilence among My people, and My people who are called by My name humble themselves and pray and seek My face and turn from their wicked ways, then I will hear from heaven, will forgive their sin and will heal their land." (2 Chronicles 7:13–14)

If Israel rebelled against God, then He would withhold rain and allow locusts to destroy their crops and pestilence to afflict the people. But the Lord also promised that if His people would humble themselves, turn from their wicked ways, and pray to Him, then He would respond by reversing the curse and healing their nation. This situation shows that when a multitude of people repent and sincerely pray, it moves His heart to answer their request.

When the Lord sent Jonah to announce His judgment on Nineveh, the king of Nineveh humbled himself before God, took off his robe and put on sackcloth as an act of repentance. He made this proclamation:

> "Both man and beast must be covered with sackcloth; and let men call on God earnestly that each may turn from his wicked way and from the violence which is in his hands. Who knows, God may turn and relent and withdraw His burning anger so that we will not perish." (Jonah 3:8–9)

The Lord was moved by this great number of people who repented of their sins and prayed for His mercy. "When God saw their deeds, that they turned from their wicked way, then God relented concerning the calamity which He had declared He would bring upon them. And He did not do it" (Jonah 3:10).

Although you certainly should let others know about your urgent prayer requests, it will be even more effective if you ask upright people who walk with God to pray for you. Since they are completely dependent on Him, their prayers will touch His heart. The Bible makes this promise: "The LORD gives grace and glory. No good thing does He withhold from *those who walk uprightly*" (Psalm 84:11).

Even so, don't assume that every request requires a certain number of people to pray, or that you have to be sinless before the Lord will hear you. God is merciful and will answer the prayers of those who desperately call out to Him. "The LORD is near to all who call upon Him, to all who call upon Him in truth" (Psalm 145:18).

18 | IF I PRAY WITHOUT CEASING, WHEN DO I SLEEP?

"Pray without ceasing." (1 Thessalonians 5:17)

How in the world can you pray without stopping? Is it even possible to "pray at all times" (Ephesians 6:18)? Does this mean you never sleep? You don't work? You can't do anything else but pray? Before you freak out, take a deep breath and settle down. It's not what you think.

Praying without ceasing does not mean you have to quit doing everything else. It means staying in touch with God throughout the day. I know some people who are continually texting and talking on their cell phones every waking moment. No one forces them to do this, and they'll even pay hundreds of dollars each month for the privilege. They love to do it because they *want* to stay in touch with others. You can do the same with your Father in heaven.

We're talking about a conversational approach to praying. God is an invisible friend who wants to hear what's on your heart and advise you as you go through each day. Jesus said, "I have called you friends, for all things that I have heard from My Father I have made known to you" (John 15:15). A friend is a person who cares about what happens to you.

Stop counting the number of minutes you're praying. You're spending quality time with the One who created you and saved you. Although you can't see God now, one day your faith will become sight the moment you leave this world and see Him face to face.

Begin your day by talking with Him when you get up in the morning. King David said, "In the morning, O LORD, You will hear my voice; in the morning I will order my prayer to You and eagerly watch" (Psalm 5:3). It's good to find a quiet place where you can be alone.

Even Jesus needed to get away from distractions to talk with His Father. "Jesus Himself would often slip away to the wilderness and pray" (Luke 5:16). Your "wilderness" is a private place where no one will disturb you.

Jesus said, "But you, when you pray, go into your inner room, close your door and pray to your Father who is in secret, and your Father who sees what is done in secret will reward you" (Matthew 6:6). In that day, the "inner room" of a house was a small storage closet with just enough room for one person. Jesus said to enter this room and close the door to shut out disturbances. As you probably know, it only takes a small noise or interruption to divert your attention away from God.

But you can't spend your entire day in your "inner room." You have many things to do during the day, so you can keep communicating with the Lord as you drive your car and as you do your work. Instead of growing impatient while you're waiting at a stop light or in a grocery line, use that time to pray for others. Praying during your daily routine should include thanking God, interceding for others, asking Him to guide you, and asking for wisdom to handle the problems you encounter.

How can you talk to God all day long without running out of things to say? The answer is found in learning to implement different kinds of prayer.

FOUR KINDS OF PRAYER

ADORATION

The way you adore God is through worship and praise. Worship is expressing to God how much you love Him, while praise is exalting

Him. The greatest commandment in the Bible is "You shall love the Lord your God with all your heart, and with all your soul, and with all your mind" (Matthew 22:37). If you truly love someone, you will express it with words. Have you ever told Him, "Lord, I love you"? Worship and praise can both be done through singing and praying passionately from your heart.

When the apostles Paul and Silas were arrested for preaching about Jesus, they were beaten and thrown into prison. Even though they were bleeding and bruised, "Paul and Silas were praying and singing hymns of praise to God" (Acts 16:25). While they were praising the Lord, an earthquake opened the prison doors and unfastened the prisoners' chains. Their praise started a chain reaction!

Do you think they would have been set free if they had been griping about their situation? I don't think so. When we stop complaining about our circumstances and start praising God instead, our spiritual chains of fear, discontentment, depression, and doubt will fall off. When the Lord heard them praising Him during their hopeless situation, it pleased Him so much that He changed their circumstances for the better. It's amazing what praising God will do.

Some days, praising and worshipping God will make you want to jump and shout. Other days, you might feel much more subdued and calm in the Lord's presence. Don't be discouraged on the days when you don't feel like praising with excitement. Adoration can also mean giving your quiet attention to God. As you go through the day, you can worship Jesus by telling Him how much you love Him.

Petition

Petition, or supplication, means asking God to supply something you need. All of our concerns, no matter how small they may seem, can be offered to God as petitions. "Be anxious for nothing, but in everything by prayer and supplication with thanksgiving let your requests be made known to God" (Philippians 4:6).

God loves for us to bring our requests to Him. The prayer of petition is probably the most common prayer because we're primarily concerned about our own needs. The Lord cares about everything that concerns us and gave us the privilege of prayer so that we will ask Him to supply what we need. Petition is covered in detail in other chapters in this book concerning provision, protection, and healing.

INTERCESSION

Intercession is praying for others that God will intervene in their lives and meet their needs. Paul instructed Timothy, "I urge, then, first of all, that petitions, prayers, intercession and thanksgiving be made for all people" (1 Timothy 2:1 NIV). We often put this type of prayer last, asking God for our own needs first, and maybe later asking for the needs of others. But intercession is a high-priority kind of prayer mentioned by Paul. Interceding for others may be the very thing that changes their hearts and turns their circumstances around. Never underestimate the power of intercessory prayer. You can read more about intercession in the chapter "Praying for Others."

THANKSGIVING

Thanksgiving is probably the most ignored prayer. The Lord wants to be thanked because it shows how much we appreciate what He has done for us. Paul told the Thessalonians, "In everything give thanks; for this is God's will for you in Christ Jesus" (1 Thessalonians 5:18). Many people aren't thankful because they're blind to all the blessings in their lives.

Bill Gates, the co-founder of Microsoft, once spoke at a convention in Seattle. At the time, Gates was the richest man in America with a personal wealth of 35 billion dollars. At the end of his speech, he allowed the audience to ask questions. One man asked, "Mr. Gates, if you were blind, would you trade all your money to have your sight restored?"

Gates said that he would indeed exchange all his money to regain his eyesight. He put a 35 billion dollar price tag on his ability to see.

If you have eyesight, have you ever thanked God for it? According to Bill Gates, it's worth 35 billion dollars—and I think he priced it too low. It's so easy to take our blessings for granted. Over 90 percent of the world's population would be thrilled to change places with you right now, no questions asked. Robert Orben has said, "The next time you feel like complaining, just remember that your garbage disposal eats better than 30 percent of the world."

The danger of being surrounded by so many blessings is that you fail to appreciate all that you have. Thankfulness is cultivated by becoming aware of everything you have and voicing your appreciation of it. You become *aware* by realizing all the blessings you have and not taking them for granted. You become *appreciative* by understanding their value and realizing what your life would be like without them. If you aren't aware of what you have, you won't be thankful. And if you don't appreciate what you have, you won't be grateful.

Thankfulness is cultivated by becoming aware of everything you have and voicing your appreciation of it.

Let's see . . . do you have *anything* to be thankful for? Yes, and much more than you realize. Listed below are some commonly ignored blessings that I thank God for daily. Not everything on my list may apply to you, so you'll need to create your own thankfulness list. Just make sure that you're sincerely grateful from your heart.

- *Salvation.* If Jesus has saved you for all eternity, how can you not thank Him every day? I thank Him for dying for my sins, giving me eternal life, and changing my destiny. This is usually the first thing I thank Him for each morning.

- *Another day of life.* You will only live for a limited time on earth. Once you die you cannot come back and have another chance to live differently, so do it right the first time. This is the first day of the rest of your life. It could also be the last day of the rest of your life. Thank Him for the privilege of living *this* day. Ask Him to show you how you can live to be pleasing to Him.

- *Family.* I thank God every day for the wife He has given me and for my children and grandchildren. If you're single, thank Him for the freedom of your singleness. Thank Him for your entire family.

- *Health.* If you're sick, ask the Lord to heal you. If you're healthy, thank the Lord every day that you're well. Jesus healed ten lepers but only one returned to thank Him. When we forget to be thankful for good health, we are like those other nine inconsiderate lepers who didn't care enough to utter the words "thank you."

- *The roof over your head.* Count yourself blessed to have shelter. What if you had to live outside in the cold or rain, the way many people do?

- *Air conditioning and heating.* Turn a dial or push a button and the room temperature changes to make you comfortable. You may take it for granted, but many people around the world sweat or shiver all night long trying to sleep because they don't have air conditioning or heat. Have you ever thanked God for these comforts?

- *Hot and cold running water.* People in many countries don't have plumbing in their homes, much less heated water for showers and baths. Every time I take a shower I thank the Lord for the hot water, soap, and towel.

- *Toilets.* What an incredible privilege it is to have indoor toilets. Until recently, most people since the creation of the earth never had this blessing. On cold, wintry evenings they had to go outside to a hole in the ground or an outhouse. Remember this the next time you go to the bathroom in the middle of the night. And yes, you should thank God for your toilet!

- *Clean water.* Many people in the world drink dirty, contaminated water, filled with parasites and bacteria. I once watched a documentary of a man who was lost at sea on a raft for several weeks before being rescued. He said, "I was so thirsty that I would have cut off my hand for a glass of water." Don't you think he was thankful when he had his first drink of water after his rescue? Remember this the next time you lift a glass of water to your lips.

- *Clothes.* While many people in the world yearn for clothing to keep warm, you might have more than you need and choose your clothes based on the latest fashions. You don't need to feel guilty about having a nice wardrobe, but you do need to remember to thank God and be extremely generous to those who are less fortunate.

- *Electricity.* Never take this luxury for granted. This power source is necessary for your TV, internet, and all your modern conveniences to operate. You don't have to bother with lanterns and candles. Do you thank God for this blessing? I do all the time.

- *Medicine and hospitals.* It's amazing how many medicines have been invented to treat illnesses and keep us in good health. You probably live near a hospital or clinic where you can get medical assistance, something that wasn't possible throughout most of the world's history. Don't take it for granted.

- *Toothpaste.* Thank the Lord for toothpaste? Yep. If you didn't have it, like many people around the world, you would have numerous cavities and other painful dental problems.

- *Eyeglasses.* When Isaac was old, "his eyes were too dim to see" (Genesis 27:1). He needed an optometrist to prescribe him a pair of glasses, but that wouldn't be possible for a few thousand years. We live in a time when it's possible to live normally despite vision problems and we need to thank God for it.

- *Refrigerators, freezers, stoves, slow cookers, and microwaves.* You have the most modern ways to preserve and prepare your food. You don't have to chop wood every day so you can cook over an open fire. Thank the Lord for these luxuries.

- *Fresh and prepared foods.* When you go to the grocery store, you can select from nearly every kind of food imaginable. You don't have to grow your own groceries. Your area of the country might not produce bananas, pineapples, or mangoes, but these fruits are brought to you from great distances and foreign countries for your enjoyment. Thank God for the labor of all of the people who planted, harvested, and transported the crops that go into your meals. Thank Him for fresh fruit, vegetables, fish, beef, and even live lobsters. If you go to the frozen food section, you can choose food that's already prepared for you. When I'm at the grocery store with my wife I'll often say, "Look at all this! Kings and emperors in the past never lived as well as we do!"

- *Restaurants.* What kind of food would you like to eat? Chinese, Japanese, Mexican, Italian, or American? Fast food or romantic dinner? Just take your pick where you want to eat. When you eat out, thank God for the food instead of complaining about the slow service. Rather than giving thanks once for a meal before you eat, why not try thanking Him throughout the entire meal as you eat it?

- *Cars.* Complaining about your car? Most people in the world don't have their own automobiles. Swap places with one of the millions of people around the world who would love to have your clunker, and you can ride a burro or a bicycle to your next destination. Thank God for your vehicle if it can take you from point A to point B. Every time I fill up my car I thank Him for the gasoline, no matter what the price per gallon may be.

- *Music.* Do you thank God for music? For Christian music? You have the finest musicians and singers in the world entertaining you on your smart phone, car radio, CD player, or computer. If you don't like a particular song, just press a button and you can hear a different one. You have more entertainment available to you than any of the kings who have lived in the past.

- *Bibles, Christian books, and online teaching ministries.* In centuries past, scribes had to slowly and carefully copy the Scriptures by hand. Making one copy of the Bible could take years. You might own several copies of God's Word, but in the past, a single complete copy would have been a priceless treasure. Have you even read the entire Book one time? In addition to the Bible, Christian books bring you information from godly teachers to help you in every area of your spiritual walk. And today, online Christian ministries can literally teach God's Word to anyone in the world who has internet access. Thank God for giving you the chance to read and be nourished by His written Word.

- *Your job.* If you are employed, God has given you the ability to earn money so that you can pay your bills and buy the things you need (see Deuteronomy 8:18). He's the one who provided your job, so thank Him for it rather than complaining about your work conditions.

The richest kings throughout the history of the world didn't have access to the gadgets and conveniences that are available to you today. When you go shopping at the grocery store, you should be shouting "Hallelujah!" as you push your cart down the aisle instead of complaining that the checkout line is too slow.

Here's an exercise that I challenge you to try. Every time that your hand touches something today, stop and think what it would be like to *not* have that item. You try to open your refrigerator and it disappears. The same thing happens with the kitchen faucet, toilet, light switch, and remote for your television. By the end of the day you will be acutely aware of hundreds of blessings that you never really noticed or appreciated before.

When you give genuine thanks to God each day, you'll discover that thankfulness is so powerful that it will drive away depression, self-pity, and complaining. And if you'll make a habit of appreciating every day as a gift from God, you can also experience a new level of joy in being thankful for everything you have.

19 | HOW ARE WE TO PRAY IN RESTAURANTS?

> "Whether, then, you eat or drink or whatever you
> do, do all to the glory of God." (1 Corinthians 10:31)

One day I went to the post office to mail a letter. A man standing near the front door was praying loudly at the top of his voice, as if he were mad at someone. Then he stopped and, with a scowl on his face, pointed his finger at the people walking into the post office. He yelled, "Are *you* going to join me in praying? Who has the courage to stand with me?"

I'm sure that he thought he was setting an example for others to follow. But it wasn't a good example. He was drawing attention to himself rather than to God, and trying to intimidate people and make them feel guilty for not praying the way he did.

The primary reason we pray is to enjoy fellowship with God— not to make a public display to show off our spirituality. The self-righteous Pharisees prayed out loud on street corners and in the marketplace so everyone would know how dedicated they were. They said their prayers, not to talk with God, but to set an example for others. The danger of praying out loud in public is that it can subtly change our attitude of prayer into a desire for others to notice our piety.

This raises a question that I've never read in a book or heard in a sermon. How are we supposed to pray when we eat in a restaurant?

Does God expect us to join hands together and have a prayer meeting? Will He get angry if we do it in a different way?

I've known people who have prayed long prayers in restaurants about everything under the sun, but forgot to thank God for the food. I've even seen people say a prayer before eating and then a few minutes later say, "Let's pray for the meal." They didn't remember the prayer they had just said!

HOW ARE WE TO PRAY IN FRONT OF UNBELIEVERS?

Please understand that I'm not saying it's always wrong to pray in public, but we should use wisdom when others are present. I've often felt uneasy when someone at the table says a long prayer as the waitress is trying to serve our food. Some people think they must pray in restaurants to set an example to others eating at the establishment. They assume that they must bow their heads and talk out loud as a way to witness to the waiters and people dining nearby.

Although we should earnestly pray for lost people to be saved, I've never seen anyone in a restaurant fall to their knees in repentance by watching a customer pray over a meal. Jesus rebuked the Pharisees for praying in order to be seen by other people. Don't confuse praying with evangelism. They're not the same. Evangelism is sharing your faith with others, while prayer is sharing fellowship with God. The Lord wants us to be thankful to Him for the food, and that can be done when we pray silently.

If you go out to eat with a group of people who don't know Christ, are you supposed to bow your head and pray in front of them? In my opinion, it's probably best to just pray silently. God can still hear you even when you don't verbalize your prayers. "The LORD knows the thoughts of man" (Psalm 94:11). In the Old Testament, God answered Hannah's prayer to have a child, even though she prayed silently. "As for Hannah, she was speaking in her heart, only her lips were moving, but her voice was not heard" (1 Samuel 1:13).

Let's take the religion out of praying. Never forget that the Lord is your audience, and not the people surrounding you. God won't get mad at you if you don't pray out loud. He just wants you to be genuinely grateful for your meal.

If you bow your head to pray when you are dining with unbelievers, they may assume that you're trying to make them feel guilty. It may even cut off your opportunity to share your faith with them at a future time. They could think that you're forcing your religion down their throats, although that's not your intent at all.

There's a story about a woman who had a sick pet. Every time she tried to force a tablespoon of medicine down its throat, the dog resisted and pulled away. One day she accidentally knocked over the bottle and the medicine spilled all over the floor. To her surprise, the dog walked over to the puddle and lapped it up. The dog wasn't against the medicine, but it was resisting the owner trying to force it down its throat.

We need to be sensitive to the Holy Spirit's guidance about how we should present Jesus to others. If we are truly interested in our friends coming to Christ, we will wisely choose the best way to communicate the gospel with them. A farmer doesn't force seeds into the hard ground, but will plow up the soil before he plants. People's hearts need to be open before we can effectively share the gospel with them. It's far more important to pray for their salvation when you're *not* in a restaurant than to publicly pray in front of them before a meal.

THERE ARE NO RULES FOR PRAYING A CERTAIN WAY.

Are we supposed to pray out loud or silently? Eyes open or eyes closed? Head bowed or head in normal position? You've probably assumed that the most appropriate way to pray in public is with your eyes closed and your head bowed. But there are no rules stating we must pray in a certain way. It might be the situation that determines how we pray.

Before Jesus fed the multitude, He prayed over the bread and fish. "And He took the five loaves and the two fish, and looking up toward heaven, He blessed the food and broke the loaves and He kept giving them to the disciples to set before them; and He divided up the two fish among them all" (Mark 6:41). Here we see Jesus praying before the meal, but this wasn't a restaurant. These people had chosen to follow Him there. He was about to feed a crowd of five thousand people, so He prayed to give thanks and multiply the food.

Notice how the Scripture says He prayed. "And *looking up* to heaven . . ."

Wait. His eyes were open and He looked up? Surely there must have been someone in that crowd of five thousand who said, "Excuse me, I hate to interrupt your prayer, but that's not the right way to pray. You're supposed to close your eyes and bow your head."

> Jesus didn't pray with His head bowed and eyes closed, but with His eyes open and His head lifted up.

We can see from Jesus' example that it's okay to pray with our eyes open. And it's not a requirement to bow our heads every time we pray. I'm not saying it's always wrong to pray in a public place, or that you can't bow your head and close your eyes. Just don't pray in this way because others are doing it and you feel obligated to do the same. Be sensitive to the Holy Spirit about whether you should or shouldn't pray publicly in restaurant.

Many times when I've been a restaurant I've bowed my head and prayed with my eyes closed. But I don't do this when the waiter is in the process of serving me. At other times, I simply looked at my plate of food and said, "Thank you, God!" It's okay to just tell God "thank you" without having to pray for twelve other things that have nothing to do with the meal.

Sometimes I'll pray silently and give thanks as I'm eating. At other times I'll eat the entire meal and, after I'm finished, say, "That was really good. Thank you, Lord for the meal." No matter which method of praying you choose, make sure that you're sincerely giving thanks.

Taking the religiosity out of praying makes it so much easier. Break from your ritual of praying the same way before every meal and let genuine thanks to God come from your heart.

Also, if you choose to pray publicly in a restaurant, make sure that you leave a generous tip because your waiter will know that you believe in God. Since servers aren't paid well, consider your tip as a charitable gift to help someone who is working to make ends meet. And if you put a gospel tract on the table for the waiter, be sure to leave an especially generous tip. That's called being a good witness.

PART 3

PRAYING SPECIFIC REQUESTS

20 | PRAYING TO BE SAVED

"Whoever will call upon the name of the
Lord will be saved." (Romans 10:13)

One evening in March 2002, a Romanian woman who worked on a *Norway* cruise ship fell overboard into the Atlantic Ocean. She didn't know how to swim. No one saw her fall into the water, but the crew realized she was missing when she didn't report for a roll call.

The captain had a crucial decision to make. Should he turn the ship around and search for her, based on the assumption that she fell overboard? If she was still on board somewhere, he would look like a fool for changing course. Perhaps it would be better to keep the passengers happy and continue on to the Virgin Islands.

After considering his options, the captain decided to turn the ship around and search for her floating body. He had to calculate how much the currents would have caused her to drift, which was about four miles off the ship's original path.

Nearly five hours later, the passengers gathered on the deck to look for her body. Suddenly someone spotted her head bobbing in the water and shouted, "There she is. She's alive!" Even though she didn't know how to swim, she had dog-paddled from 12:30 a.m. until 10:30 the next morning! Against all odds of survival, the woman was rescued.[16]

Consider the hopelessness this woman felt when she plunged into the dark waters of the Atlantic. Swap places with her for a moment. Picture yourself alone in the middle of the Atlantic Ocean at night, hundreds of miles from shore. You're in the most hopeless, desperate situation of your life. You can't swim, so you frantically dog-paddle to keep yourself from drowning.

The lights of the ship move into the distance and slowly disappear. Now you're in pitch darkness. Fear strikes your heart when you realize this is how your life will end. In just a matter of minutes, or hours at best, you'll either be eaten by sharks or will run out of strength and drown.

In sheer desperation, you call out to God to save you.

Lord, I realize that I've lived only for myself, but if you will save me from drowning, I'll live the rest of my life for you. My only hope is for the ship to come back and miraculously find me. Please let that happen!

You continue treading water throughout the night until the sun comes up. You don't know how much longer you can endure. Then, after surviving in the ocean for ten hours, you can't believe your eyes—the ship has come back looking for you!

You're merely a dot in a huge ocean of waves, so the odds against them finding you are astronomical. But then a passenger sees your head above the water, which leads to your rescue.

Now I want you to consider a situation that's far more serious than this one. You're currently drowning in a sea of sin, and it's impossible for you to save yourself. If you go under, you'll spend all eternity in darkness and torment away from God's presence. You only have one hope of being saved—if a Savior comes searching for you.

And this is why Jesus came from heaven to earth. He searches for lost people who want to be saved. He said, "The Son of Man has come to seek and to save that which was lost" (Luke 19:10). He's ready and willing to save anyone who will call out to Him.

God's Plan of Salvation

When I was a boy, I desperately wanted someone to explain to me how I could go to heaven when I died. Our family didn't attend church except for a few times a year, and even then I didn't hear anyone talk about being saved. It wasn't until I was a senior in high school that someone explained to me God's plan of salvation. I've summarized it in the following four points with Scripture.

1. The Problem—Sin separates us from God.

Sin is what keeps us away from God. "But your iniquities have made a separation between you and your God, and your sins have hidden His face from you so that He does not hear" (Isaiah 59:2). We commit sins against God with every wrong thought, word, and deed.

Let's say that a really "good" person only commits three sins a day. That doesn't sound so bad, but that's over a thousand sins a year, and can be over 70,000 sins in a lifetime. And it only takes *one* sin to separate us from God. No one is exempt: "For all have sinned and fall short of the glory of God" (Romans 3:23). If something doesn't happen to remove every sin from our lives and turn our hearts around, we will remain separated from God forever and will have no hope of ever going to heaven.

2. The Solution—Jesus died on the cross for your sins.

"But God demonstrates His own love toward us, in that while we were yet sinners, Christ died for us. . . . For the wages of sin is death, but the free gift of God is eternal life in Christ Jesus our Lord" (Romans 5:8, 6:23).

Jesus didn't pay the price for only a select few. He died for everyone in the world—including you. As God in a human body, He offered Himself to pay what was owed for every sin that has ever been committed. "He Himself is the propitiation for our sins; and not for ours only, but also for those of the whole world" (1 John 2:2). His death on the cross made it possible for you to be saved.

Everyone wants to be saved from hell, but few want to be saved from their sins. The angel who announced Jesus's birth said, "You shall call His name Jesus, for He will save His people *from their sins*"

(Matthew 1:23). Jesus paid the price to cleanse your sins and forgive you. If you choose to reject Him, you will pay for your own sins in hell and the debt will never be paid off. But when you are saved by Jesus from your sins, then you'll also be saved from punishment in hell and given eternal life with Him.

3. THE OFFER—SALVATION IS A FREE GIFT THAT'S OFFERED TO YOU.

"For it is by grace you have been saved, through faith—and this is not from yourselves, it is the gift of God—not by works, so that no one can boast" (Ephesians 2:8–9 NIV). You can't do anything to earn a gift. If you try to work for it as though you could earn it, then it ceases being a gift and becomes a wage. God offers the gift of eternal life to everyone because He wants everyone to be saved (1 Timothy 2:4).

"Grace" means "undeserved favor." You are not saved by your faith, but by God's grace. Your faith is the way you *receive* His free gift of salvation and forgiveness of your sins. It's not a matter of having "enough" faith. Don't focus your attention on your own faith but on His grace. Having child-like faith means trusting that God will do what He says.

4. THE DECISION—YOU MUST RECEIVE JESUS AND HIS GIFT OF SALVATION.

"But as many as received Him [Jesus], to them He gave the right to become children of God, even to those who believe in His name" (John 1:12). If someone purchases a gift for you, it's potentially yours. But it doesn't actually become yours until you reach out and receive it. The way you receive Jesus's gift of eternal life is by calling out to Him to save you.

I've heard some people say that there's no "prayer of salvation" in the Bible. Yes, there is. "Whoever will call on the name of the Lord will be saved" (Romans 10:13; cf. Acts 2:21; Joel 2:32). Calling out to the Lord is a prayer. If you're drowning, you'll desperately cry out for someone to save you. In the same way, when you realize you're headed for an eternity away from God because your sins aren't forgiven, you'll plead with Him to be saved.

You can receive Jesus Christ by sincerely praying the following prayer. Pray it with the same desperation as if you were treading water at night in the middle of the Atlantic Ocean.

PRAYER TO BE SAVED

Heavenly Father, I have sinned against you and ask for you to have mercy on me. I believe that Jesus paid for my sins on the cross and rose from the dead. Please forgive me for every sin I have committed and will commit in the future. Jesus, come into my heart and save me. I give my life to you and ask for you to live through me. Thank you for giving me eternal life.

If you sincerely prayed this prayer, you are now a child of God. All your sins are forgiven and you now have eternal life. The Scripture says, "These things I have written to you who believe in the name of the Son of God, so that *you may know* that you have eternal life" (1 John 5:13). God makes this promise to all who have received Jesus: "Their sins and their lawless deeds I will remember no more" (Hebrews 10:17).

Welcome to the family of God!

21 | PRAYING FOR GOD'S PROVISION

"Give us this day our daily bread." (Matthew 6:11)

As already mentioned in Chapter 5, we've got to stop trying to figure out how God will answer our prayers. The following true story shows that the Lord hears our requests and can use the most unlikely means to deliver the provision we need.

While crossing the Atlantic on a ship many years ago, Bible teacher and author F. B. Meyer was asked to speak to the passengers. An agnostic listened to Meyer's message about answered prayer and told a friend, "I didn't believe a word of it."

Later that same day, the agnostic went to hear Meyer speak to another group of passengers. But before he went to the meeting, he put two oranges in his pocket. On his way, he passed an elderly woman who was fast asleep in her deck chair. Her arms were outstretched and her hands were wide open, so as a joke he put the two oranges in her palms. After the meeting, he saw the elderly woman eating the fruit.

"You seem to be enjoying that orange," he remarked with a smile.

"Yes, sir," she replied. "My Father is very good to me."

"What do you mean?" pressed the agnostic.

She explained, "I have been seasick for days. I was asking God somehow to send me an orange. I fell asleep while I was praying. When I awoke, I found He had sent me not only one but two oranges!"[17]

The agnostic was stunned because he had just heard Meyer talk about how the Lord answers prayer. God humorously chose to use a man who was skeptical about answered prayer to answer a woman's prayer. As a result of this incident, he gave his life to the Lord.

God hears us when we call out to Him for provision and will give us what we need to make it through each day. Jesus taught us to pray, "Give us this day our daily bread." He didn't teach us to ask for yearly bread because He wants us to trust Him for provision every day. As we discussed earlier, the third purpose of prayer is to show God how seriously we want the things we request and trust Him to provide them. If He gave us everything we needed at one time, we would have no reason to keep depending on Him.

A wealthy father promised his son an annual allowance. On a certain day each year he gave his son a large amount of cash. After the son collected his money, the only time the father saw him was the next year on the day he received his allowance.

The father decided to change the plan. Instead of giving his son a huge amount of money once a year, he distributed it on a daily basis. From then on, he saw his son every day.

We're a lot like that son. If everything comes to us easily, we won't appreciate how we got it. But if provision is connected to our relationship with God, we will be thankful for the daily blessings He gives us.

In Jesus's day people didn't have fully stocked grocery stores and a variety of restaurants on every corner like we have today. The fear of starvation was at the forefront of their minds every day. People at that time never knew where their next meal was coming from and literally had to trust God to provide daily food.

It certainly seems as though most of us today don't need to trust the Lord to provide our daily bread. We have canned food in our cupboards, frozen food in our freezers, and fresh food in our refrigerators. A pizza is a phone call away and can be delivered to your door. American families with lower incomes are able to feed their families through the government's Supplemental Nutrition Assistance Program (SNAP) and free public school meal plans. All this food is available to nearly everyone—and without even having to say one word in prayer.

So why should we pray, "Give us this day our daily bread"? Does this prayer even apply to us today?

Of course, this verse applies to every generation. We still need to ask God for daily bread because He wants us to rely on Him to provide all our needs. When Jesus sent His disciples to preach in several cities, He told them, "Take nothing for your trip, neither a walking stick, bag, bread, money, or extra clothes" (Luke 9:3 NCV). Why would He tell them not to take anything? No food? No money? What's wrong with taking along some supplies?

This was a unique situation because Jesus wanted them to depend completely on God for their daily bread. If they would pray and do what He asked, their every need would be met. Later, shortly before Jesus was betrayed, He asked His disciples to recall this time when He had sent them out empty-handed: "And He said to them, 'When I sent you out without money belt and bag and sandals, you did not lack anything, did you?' They said, 'No, nothing'" (Luke 22:35).

Jesus knew that His Father in heaven would provide for them, and the disciples all testified that they didn't lack anything they needed. He knew this would be recorded in the Scriptures for all to read about God's faithfulness to provide.

What is meant by "daily bread"?

After the Israelites left Egypt, they lived in the wilderness for forty years. The only way they survived was by the Lord sending them bread from heaven every morning. The bread, called manna, would miraculously appear on the ground every day and all they had to do was gather it up. (The word *manna* means, "What is it?")

Behold, on the surface of the wilderness there was a fine flake-like thing, fine as the frost on the ground. When the sons of Israel saw it, they said to one another, "*What is it?*" For they did not know what it was. And Moses said to them, "It is the bread which the LORD has given you to eat. . . ." They gathered it morning by morning, every man as much as he should eat. (Exodus 16:14–15, 21)

The Lord told them to gather up enough for just one day because He wanted them to trust Him for their daily provision. This was an object lesson for future generations as well. God had the Israelites put a jar of manna into the Ark of the Covenant "to be kept throughout your generations" as a reminder that He would continue to provide for their daily needs (Exodus 16:33–34).

After Israel entered the Promised Land and ate the crops in the land of Canaan, God changed the way He provided for them. "The manna ceased on the day after they had eaten some of the produce of the land, so that the sons of Israel no longer had manna, but they ate some of the yield of the land of Canaan during that year" (Joshua 5:12).

HOW DOES GOD SEND "DAILY BREAD" TODAY?

The Lord exists outside of time, but He deals with us on a daily basis. "Through the LORD's mercies we are not consumed because His compassions fail not. They are *new every morning*" (Lamentations 3:22–23). Each day is a new start in the realm of time.

It only makes sense that if Jesus instructs us to pray for *daily* bread, we must pray for His provision *every day*. Obviously, it takes more than bread to keep us alive. Jesus said, "Man shall not live by *bread alone* but on every word that proceeds out of the mouth of God" (Matthew 4:4). "Daily bread" certainly means food, but it also includes everything else that we need to live each day.

It only makes sense that if Jesus instructs us to pray for *daily* bread, we must pray for provision *every day*.

When you ask God to provide money to pay a bill, you won't find a bundle of cash the next morning laying on your front yard, like the manna He sent to the Israelites in the wilderness. Sometimes His provision comes in ways that don't look supernatural. Jesus told His followers, "Look at the birds of the air, that they do not sow, nor reap nor gather into barns, and yet your heavenly Father feeds them. Are you not worth much more than they?" (Matthew 6:26).

Jesus probably pointed to some birds and said, "Do you see those birds on that tree branch? They aren't worried about starving to death, because your heavenly Father feeds them."

How does God take responsibility for feeding every bird in the entire world? I've never seen a hand coming down from heaven dropping worms into open beaks. If He doesn't feed them in that way, He must use a different method to give them food. He does it by showing them where to find worms, bugs, and seeds. And this shows His faithfulness because you've never seen a bird starve to death.[18]

Then Jesus drove home His point to those who were worried about where to find their daily bread: "You are worth more than birds." If the Lord cares for birds, won't He also provide for His children, who are far more valuable?

How does God provide for us today?

Each person's daily bread is a unique provision because we all have different needs. God usually answers our prayers for provision in these three ways.

1. God can provide for you by using other people.

The Lord will use a variety of resources to answer your prayers. Jesus said, "Give, and it will be given to you. They will pour into your lap a good measure—pressed down, shaken together, and running over" (Luke 6:38). He said "they" will pour this abundance into your lap, which means He will use different people and other sources to bring provision to you.

When Elijah needed food during a drought, God told him, "Arise, go to Zarephath . . . behold, *I have commanded a widow* there to provide for you" (1 Kings 17:9). The Lord didn't speak to a rich person to help Elijah, but instead commanded a poor woman who was down to her last meal. When Elijah arrived there, she seemed to be unaware that God had commanded her to provide for him. This shows that God can command people to deliver His provision to you, even if they are unaware that they are fulfilling His purposes.

> God can command people to deliver His provision to you, even if they are unaware that they are fulfilling His purposes.

She had planned to eat "the last supper" with her son until Elijah asked for it. She gave her last bit of flour and oil to Elijah instead of keeping it for herself (1 Kings 17:10–24). The Lord rewarded this woman for giving her last meal to the prophet by supernaturally multiplying her flour and oil throughout the rest of the drought (1 Kings 17:14–16).

2. GOD CAN PROVIDE FOR YOU IN MIRACULOUS WAYS.

Peter was a fisherman before he became a disciple of Jesus. After fishing all night in the Sea of Galilee and catching nothing, Jesus told him to go back out and drop the nets again. This time he filled up two boats with so many fish that they started to sink (Luke 5:1–7). Jesus could have stopped sending fish into his nets before the boats started sinking. But He did this miracle to help Peter realize that God could provide more than he expected or needed. If Jesus could make this many fish obey Him, then He could do whatever was necessary to provide for his every need. It was a no-brainer—Peter left his fishing business to follow Jesus.

Later, Peter was standing outside of a house in Capernaum when the tax collectors arrived. They asked Peter if Jesus would pay the tax to support the temple (see Exodus 30:13). When Peter went into the house to tell Him about their request, Jesus spoke to him first about the tax. Even though Jesus wasn't outside to hear the conversation, He spoke first to show Peter that already knew what they wanted before he could say anything.

And the way He provided the money for the tax was even more amazing. Jesus told Peter, "Go to the sea and throw in a hook, and take the first fish that comes up; and when you open its mouth, you will find a shekel. Take that and give it to them for you and Me" (Matthew 17:27).

In the previous miracle, Jesus had proven that He could provide by making *hundreds* of fish swim into Peter's net. Now He would show Peter His ability to control *just one* fish to do what He needed. Tens of thousands of fish were swimming in the Sea of Galilee, but God made sure that the only fish with a coin in its mouth would go to the right spot to bite on Peter's hook. When he caught the fish, he opened its mouth and found a coin, which was the exact amount needed to pay the tax.

This shows that the Lord knows exactly what you need and can provide for you in unusual ways, even if the odds look humanly impossible. If you've been praying to meet the right person to marry, remember Peter catching this fish. If God can lead a fish to a man, He can lead a woman to a man, or a man to a woman. The Lord will take care of matching you with the right person—just like He made the right fish bite on Peter's hook.[19] If you ask God to provide for an urgent need in your life, He can lead someone to bring the provision to you at the right time.

In another example of God's miraculous provision, He commanded ravens to provide for Elijah. This prophet "prayed earnestly that it might not rain, and it did not rain on the earth for three years and six months" (James 5:17). Most people pray that it will rain, but Elijah prayed that it wouldn't rain so that wicked King Ahab and his wife Jezebel would repent.

Elijah would also have to suffer through the three-year drought. Sometimes God will allow a country go through difficult times as a wakeup call so the people will repent of their sins and surrender their lives to Him. But even if a nation goes into an economic depression or another crisis, He still promises to provide for His people.

The Lord told Elijah to go to the brook Cherith. " 'It shall be that you will drink of the brook, and *I have commanded the ravens* to provide for you there.' ... The ravens brought him bread and meat in the morning and bread and meat in the evening, and he would drink from the brook" (1 Kings 17:4, 6).

God commanded the ravens to provide for Elijah. He spoke to the birds and showed them exactly where to fly to find him. The birds also knew *when* to bring him food—for breakfast and dinner. This proves that God knows exactly where you are and how to deliver His provision to you. The Lord can provide for you in ways that you would never expect.

God knows exactly where you are and
how to deliver His provision to you.

---

3. THE LORD CAN PROVIDE FOR YOU THROUGH YOUR JOB.

If you have a job, you probably get paid on a weekly, bi-weekly, or monthly schedule. How can you learn to trust God for daily provision when your paychecks come at intervals? You can show your dependence on the Lord by thanking Him every day for your job.

God not only opened the door for you to be hired at your place of employment, He also gave you the knowledge and ability to do your job. You didn't get hired because you equipped yourself with intelligence and skills. Your talents are gifts from God, who gives you the ability to gain wealth and provide income through your work.

Moses warned the people of Israel that if they didn't keep giving thanks to God for providing their daily bread, they would stop depending on Him and would become proudly self-sufficient:

In the wilderness He fed you manna which your fathers did not know, that He might humble you and that He might test you, to do good for you in the end. Otherwise, you may say in your heart, *"My power and the strength of my hand made me this wealth."* But you shall remember the LORD your God, for it is *He who is giving you power to make wealth*, that He may confirm His covenant which He swore to your fathers, as it is this day. (Deuteronomy 8:26–18)

Praying for daily bread not only keeps you dependent on God as your provider, it also keeps dreams of self-sufficiency and ungratefulness from entering your heart. So now you understand why it's so important to ask God to send bread each day.

PRAYER

Father, I realize that every good gift comes from you and all blessings flow from your throne. I ask you to provide me with what I need today. (*Be specific and tell Him about each and every need*). Thank you for the people that you have led to help me. Thank you for giving me work to do and people to care for. And thank you in advance for supplying what I need today.

22 | PRAYING FOR PROTECTION

"But the Lord is faithful, and He will strengthen and protect you from the evil one." (2 Thessalonians 3:3)

Three men were robbing a bakery and forced the cashier down on the floor behind the counter. As one man held a gun to her head, she prayed that God would protect her.

At that moment, a loud buzzer started beeping. The robbers assumed it was the burglar alarm, so they rushed out the door without harming her or taking any money. The buzzer wasn't a security alarm. It was the oven timer that signaled that the bread she was baking was ready.[20]

Coincidence, you say? Perhaps. But the Lord knew that she would be praying for help and the robbers could be scared away. So He led her to set the buzzer for just the right time when it would need to go off in order to make the crooks flee.

Just as we can pray for daily bread, we can also pray for daily protection. In this life, we are trusting in an invisible God whom we won't see until after we die. But until that day comes, we can call on Him for protection.

We live in a world where it's possible to be injured through wars, riots, violence, accidents, and evil people. We won't ever be totally exempt from all harm until we leave this present world and enter heaven. Although everyone will get hurt to some degree during their lifetime, many physical and spiritual attacks can be averted by asking for God's protection. I've been spared from numerous near-miss accidents, which I attribute to the Lord intervening and preventing the catastrophes.

Just as we can pray for daily bread,
we can also pray for daily protection.

I know a man who left his house to go to work one day, but forgot to log off the Internet on his home computer. When he came home at the end of the day, he checked the status of his firewall protection program. He was shocked to discover there had been 488 attempts to hack into his computer that day. Someone was trying to plant a virus that would secretly give the hacker complete access to all the information on his hard drive. The firewall program running in the background had protected his computer from a disaster.

Our prayers for protection are similar to running a firewall program that shields us from the spiritual attacks of the enemy. Although we are not aware of all potential dangers, God hears our prayers and works in the background to prevent many of them from happening.

In the Old Testament, when Ezra was preparing to lead a group of returning exiles through a dangerous area, he prayed for God's protection. He wrote:

> Then I proclaimed a fast there at the river of Ahava, that we might humble ourselves before our God *to seek from Him a safe journey for us, our little ones*, and all our possessions. For I was ashamed to request from the king troops and horsemen to protect us from the enemy on the way, because we had said to the king, "The hand of our God is favorably disposed to all those who seek Him, but His power and His anger are against all those who forsake Him." (Ezra 8:21–22)

Ezra didn't ask for the king's troops to protect them because he assured the king that God would take care of them. Certainly, it's perfectly fine to ask for police protection because God has ordained law enforcement to protect citizens (Romans 13:4). However, Ezra knew traveling through the enemy territory was so dangerous that only God could properly guard them. He prayed and completely trusted the Lord for protection from the enemy attacks.

After they safely arrived in Jerusalem, he wrote, "The hand of our God was over us, and He delivered us from the hand of the enemy and the ambushes by the way" (Ezra 8:31). To say it another way, God's firewall protection program worked to prevent their attempted attacks. The Lord supernaturally blocked every ambush from bandits so that the caravan arrived safely.

WHEN PROTECTION IS NOT GUARANTEED

God never promised us protection from persecution. Herod the king arrested both James and Peter. The Lord allowed James to be put to death with the sword, but He sent an angel to supernaturally set Peter free from prison (Acts 12:1–7). The Scriptures do not tell us why one disciple was killed and the other one wasn't, although we do know Peter himself later became a martyr.

Jesus knew most of His disciples would be tortured and killed for their faith, so He didn't promise safe protection from persecution. He told His followers, "*Do not fear those who kill the body* but are unable to kill the soul; but rather fear Him who is able to destroy both soul and body in hell" (Matthew 10:28). He told His followers not to be afraid—even when facing death. This life is very short and death will eventually take us in one way or another. Heaven is the place of eternal joy and thousands of times better than our greatest happiness on this earth.

God also doesn't promise us protection when we act irresponsibly. You can't drive your vehicle down the highway with your eyes closed and pray, "Lord, I trust you to protect me and guide my car to its destination." The Lord isn't going to safeguard such foolishness.

Satan tried to tempt Jesus to jump off the highest point of the temple by promising Him false protection. The devil misquoted Scripture and tried to convince Him that the angels would catch Him before He hit the ground. Jesus didn't take the bait. If He had jumped,

He would have obeyed Satan and not His Father. Even though He was the Son of God, He knew that protection wasn't promised for acting unwisely.

Praying for Protection Gives Us Peace of Mind

God wants us to live in peace and not be tormented by the fear of harm. This isn't just a nice idea; it's part of our calling as Christians. "God has called us to peace" (1 Corinthians 7:15). Jesus told His disciples, "Peace I leave with you, My peace I give to you; not as the world gives do I give to you. Let not your heart be troubled, neither let it be afraid" (John 14:27 NKJV). Worry takes over when you let your heart be troubled and afraid, but peace comes through praying and trusting God.

As you pray for the Lord's protection, remind Him of these promises He has made and trust them for your situation. Declare to Him what He has promised to you.

> Even though I walk through the valley of the shadow of death, I fear no evil, for You are with me. (Psalm 23:4)

> The LORD is the one who goes ahead of you; He will be with you. He will not fail you or forsake you. Do not fear or be dismayed. (Deuteronomy 31:8)

> God told Israel in the wilderness: I am going to send an angel before you to guard you along the way and to bring you into the place which I have prepared. (Exodus 23:20)

> You will walk in your way securely and your foot will not stumble. When you lie down, you will not be afraid; when you lie down, your sleep will be sweet. (Proverbs 3:23–24)

> In peace I will both lie down and sleep, for You alone, O LORD, make me to dwell in safety. (Psalm 4:8)

> The LORD is my light and my salvation; whom shall I fear? The LORD is the defense of my life; whom shall I dread? . . . Though a host en-

camp against me, my heart will not fear; though war arise against me, in spite of this I shall be confident. (Psalm 27:1, 3)

I will lift up my eyes to the mountains; from where shall my help come? My help comes from the LORD, who made heaven and earth. . . . The LORD will protect you from all evil; He will keep your soul. The LORD will guard your going out and your coming in from this time forth and forever. (Psalm 121:1–2, 7–8)

I will say to the LORD, "My refuge and my fortress, My God, in whom I trust!" For it is He who delivers you from the snare of the trapper and from the deadly pestilence. . . .

You will not be afraid of the terror by night, or of the arrow that flies by day; of the pestilence that stalks in darkness, or of the destruction that lays waste at noon. A thousand may fall at your side and ten thousand at your right hand, but it shall not approach you. . . .

For you have made the LORD, my refuge, even the Most High, your dwelling place. No evil will befall you, nor will any plague come near your tent. For He will give His angels charge concerning you, to guard you in all your ways. They will bear you up in their hands, that you do not strike your foot against a stone. . . .

"Because he has loved Me, therefore I will deliver him; I will set him securely on high, because he has known My name. He will call upon Me, and I will answer him; I will be with him in trouble; I will rescue him and honor him. With a long life I will satisfy him and let him see My salvation." (Psalm 91:2–3, 5–7, 9–12, 14–16)

PRAYER

Lord, I ask for your divine protection today for myself, my family, and (*name others*). I ask you to keep me and others alert as I travel. Send your angels to protect me so I will arrive safely at my destination. When I go to sleep at night, I will not worry because I trust you for protection. Station your angels around my residence and keep all possible intruders away. Thank you for protecting me. In Jesus' name.

23 | PRAYING TO GET THROUGH DEVASTATION

> "In my distress I called upon the LORD,
> Yes, I cried to my God;
> And from His temple He heard my voice,
> And my cry for help came into His ears."
> (2 Samuel 22:7)

In the television series *24*, Jack Bauer is a special agent with the Counter-Terrorism Unit. He's always involved in an undercover plan that requires him to call the President of the United States to ask permission for a highly classified assignment.

The President asks Bauer, "Jack, what exactly are you planning to do?"

Bauer answers, "Mr. President, you don't need to know and I don't have time to explain. Please, I just ask you to trust me. I promise I'll do my very best to resolve this problem." Even though the President is curious, he always gives Bauer permission because his trust in him is greater than his need to know.

Whenever we are going through a difficult situation, we'd like for God to explain why it's happening. Instead of giving us clarification, He says, "You don't need to know. I just ask you to trust Me." When you are suffering, your greatest need isn't an explanation, but comfort for your soul and the strength to endure.

Remember prayer's fourth purpose—to let go of your problems and hand them over to God. This reason to pray isn't to *get* something, but to *get through* something. "Is anyone among you suffering? Let him pray" (James 5:13 NKJV). You're going through a divorce, a loved one passed away, you've lost your job, or you're under extreme stress. You're tossing and turning at night because this ordeal is wearing you out, but where can you go to find relief for your soul?

This reason to pray isn't to *get* something, but to *get through* something.

When you come to Jesus "you will find rest for your souls" (Matthew 11:29). Prayer is how you release your burdens to the Lord so you can find peace of mind. "Let your requests be made known to God, and the peace of God, which surpasses all understanding, will guard your hearts and minds through Christ Jesus" (Philippians 4:6–7). Paul doesn't say that getting the *answer* to your request will give you peace, but just turning your request over to God is enough to calm your soul.

Over forty years ago, a Christian married couple I know, Joe and Joan, lost their seven-year-old son when a vehicle struck him. They knew the only way they could make it through this tragedy was to keep pleading to the Lord for His grace. I asked Joe how they survived.

"For a couple of weeks after the accident we couldn't even function," Joe explained. "All we could do was to cry out to God to help us. We kept praying for grace just to make it through each day. Even though we were in agony, we never blamed God for this accident."

Over the years, Joe and Joan have helped many people who were grieving over the loss of loved ones. Joe told me, "The sooner you reach out to help other people, the quicker you'll get over your own pain. You're not the only person in the world going through this. We tell the people we counsel the two things they cannot say are 'Why did this happen?' and 'What if I had done something to keep this from happening?' Those questions cannot be answered and will drive you crazy if you keep mulling them over in your mind. When you quit asking *why* and *what if*, it will help you recover and get on with your life."

Another man who lost his young child said, "You cannot think your way out of it, buy your way out of it, or work your way out of it. You can only trust your way out of it." If you are going through a similar devastation, the only way to get through it is by placing your complete trust in the Lord. Remember this verse: "The LORD is near to the brokenhearted and saves those who are crushed in spirit" (Psalm 34:18).

> "You cannot think your way out of it, buy your way out of it, or work your way out of it. You can only trust your way out of it."

Jesus didn't spend His time giving explanations about why accidents and bad things happen on earth. I've heard some people say, "Everything happens for a reason." But the Bible doesn't necessarily teach this. That idea assumes that God causes everything to happen—even evil, sin, and tragedies, which He doesn't. If a man trips and breaks his ankle, is there a divine explanation for it? Is God trying to send him a message? No. Is there a natural explanation for it? Yes, he didn't see the hole in the ground right in front of him.

Stop trying to figure out a theological reason why something did or didn't happen. "There are some things the LORD our God has kept secret, but there are some things he has let us know. These things belong to us and our children forever" (Deuteronomy 29:29 NCV).

God isn't going to answer your questions about why you're going through your present struggle in this life. However, your questions will be answered in the next life when you stand face to face with God. Everything will finally make sense when the mysteries of this life are explained. Paul writes, "For now we see in a mirror dimly, but then *face to face*; now I know in part, but *then I will know fully just as I also have been fully known*" (1 Corinthians 13:12).

During His time on earth, Jesus spoke about a couple of tragedies that had people scratching their heads. Some Galileans had been murdered by Pilate, while others were killed in an accident. Both calamities resulted in the premature ending of life—death at the hands of an evil man and death through an accident. But He never explained why either of these tragedies happened.

> Now on the same occasion there were some present who reported to Him about the Galileans whose blood Pilate had mixed with their sacrifices. And Jesus said to them, "Do you suppose that these Galileans were greater sinners than all other Galileans because they suffered this fate? I tell you, no. . . . Or do you suppose that those eighteen on whom the tower in Siloam fell and killed them were worse culprits than all the men who live in Jerusalem? I tell you, no." (Luke 13:1–5)

Pilate murdered some innocent worshippers who were offering sacrifices to God. Eighteen people lost their lives when a tower collapsed and fell on them, presumably during its construction. The Pharisees had apparently taught that these people died prematurely as punishment for their sins. Jesus corrected this incorrect assumption and said that the catastrophes hadn't happened because of their sins. Twice, He said, "I tell you, *no*." God wasn't to blame for those tragedies.

When you are praying through a devastating situation, you can find relief for your soul by keeping four things in mind.

1. Don't Blame God for Causing What You're Going Through.

Why is it that so many people who don't even believe in God want to blame Him whenever something bad happens? Directing your anger toward the Lord will only clog your pipeline for the grace and comfort that you need right now.

God doesn't cause evil to happen. That would go against His nature. Jesus said that His Father "is kind to ungrateful and evil men" (Luke 6:35). David wrote, "For the LORD is good to all" (Psalm 145:9). God only gives us what is good. "Every good thing given and every perfect gift is from above, coming down from the Father of lights" (James 1:17). These passages make it clear that God is not to blame for disasters, accidents, or actions by evil people, as if He somehow wanted people to suffer.

In the Old Testament, Job lost all his sons and daughters in a tornado and his livestock were stolen by his enemies. When he received the terrible news, Job fell to the ground and worshipped God. The Scripture says, "Through all this Job did not sin nor did he blame God" (Job 1:13–20, 22). Instead of accusing the Lord, he chose to draw near to Him for strength.

Although Job didn't understand why those things happened, the Scripture informs us that Satan had orchestrated those calamities because he wanted Job to curse God. (Don't assume that every disaster is caused by the devil. Job's trial was a unique situation.) Even Job's wife tried to get him to blame the Lord. She said to him, "Curse God and die!" (Job 2:9). Pinning the blame on God will never resolve your problem, but it will always poison you with bitterness.

When you're tempted to cut off your communication with God because of your hurt, try telling Him how you feel instead. Job didn't curse God, but he did grieve and mourn his loss, which the Lord heard. When you're grieving over your own suffering or that of others, you can appeal to God, knowing that He does not want it to last forever. The Lord's ultimate plan is to take away all suffering and end death forever. When you grieve without becoming angry at Him, you're showing Him that you understand His heart and you're looking forward to His complete redemption.

2. PRAY FOR GOD'S GRACE, COMFORT, AND STRENGTH.

When Paul asked God three times to take away his aggravating "thorn in the flesh," the Lord told him, "My grace is sufficient for you, for power is perfected in weakness" (2 Corinthians 12:9). If God doesn't deliver you from your problem, He promises to give you the grace to get through it. Paul learned to embrace God's grace to endure his difficulty.

God's grace is like a spiritual shock absorber that softens the full impact of the negative force that's trying to crush you. If you fall on a pillow on a concrete floor, you may experience some aching but the cushion shields you from the full force of the impact. The

Lord wants to comfort you in the midst of your difficulty. He is "the Father of mercies and God of all comfort, *who comforts us in all our affliction* so that we will be able to comfort those who are in any affliction with the comfort with which we ourselves are comforted by God" (2 Corinthians 1:3–4). God's supernatural peace and comfort will ease your suffering as you go through your trial.

> God's grace is like a spiritual shock absorber that softens the full impact of the negative force that's trying to crush you.

3. Ask for God's wisdom.

Perhaps you're in the intense strain of a puzzling situation and don't know what to do next. The Lord desires to give you wisdom and guide your steps. Receiving His insight and direction were covered in chapter 15, "If I pray for wisdom how do I know when I get it?"

God says, "I will instruct you and teach you in the way which you should go" (Psalm 32:8). Making your way through a difficulty starts by walking in the light the Lord has given you. He may be shining just enough light on your path to take one step. But when you take that first step by faith, He will give you more light for the next step.

When you're driving at night, you can't see down the entire highway. You're only able to see as far as your car's headlights shine down the road. But as your car moves forward, the light continues to move ahead of you. As you follow God's leading, He will light your path as you keep walking by faith in the way you should go.

4. Surrender your problem into God's hands.

When you've lost someone or something you cherish, you'll go through a grieving process as you deal with your loss. But after you've grieved for a while, you need to let go of your situation and move on with your life. Any counselor will tell you that if you grieve too long it will affect you in a negative way. It's not that you will completely forget the disturbing experience or the person you've lost when you stop grieving, but releasing your burden to God will help you get through your sorrow and receive healing.

Samuel was grieving over Saul disobeying God and being rejected as king. The Lord asked Samuel, *"How long will you grieve over Saul, since I have rejected him from being king over Israel?"* (1 Samuel 16:1). The Lord wanted Samuel to let go of the situation because He had chosen someone else to take his place.

You can hold onto a person with your hands, but you can also hold onto a person or situation with your heart. To release your problems to God means to *let go in your spirit.* It's like a trapeze artist who performs in a circus. When the trapeze bar swings her way, she must let go of the bar she's holding onto so she can grab the new bar.

To release your burden to God, you must willingly let go of your troublesome situation and place it in the Lord's hands so you can move on to the next chapter of your life. The good news is that God can handle your troubles and losses better than you can. "Cast your burden upon the Lord and He will sustain you" (Psalm 55:22). If you've lost a loved one, you can cast your care for that person on the Lord since He has told us, "I am the resurrection and the life" (John 11:25).

Yes, you will always have unanswered questions. If all your questions were answered, you wouldn't need to trust the Lord for anything. Placing your complete trust in God relieves you from having to figure everything out. Your trust in Him becomes greater than your need to understand. King Solomon wrote, "Trust in the Lord with all your heart and lean not on your own understanding. In all your ways acknowledge Him and He shall direct your paths" (Proverbs 3:5–6 NKJV).

So then, as you pray through your disappointment, remember what God wants to say to you: "You don't need to know why. I just ask you to trust Me."

Your trust in God must become greater
than your need to understand.

PRAYER

Heavenly Father, I'm going through the toughest situation in my life. I ask you to give me your grace and comfort. I receive it. Please give me the ability to accept the love and grace that people want to share with me during this terrible time. I need your strength to make it through today. I don't understand why this has happened, but I choose to trust you and I'll quit trying to figure it out. I ask for your wisdom about what I should do next and I receive it by faith. I release my problem and place it in your hands so I can move on to what you have planned next for my life.

24 | PRAYING FOR HEALING

"Therefore, confess your sins to one
another, and pray for one another so that
you may be healed." (James 5:16)

Dr. Randy Byrd was a staff cardiologist at the San Francisco General Hospital and a professor at the University of California. He conducted a ten-month study of 393 patients admitted to the coronary intensive care unit at the hospital. One hundred ninety-two of those patients were assigned to a "prayed for" group, while the remaining 201 patients were assigned to a "not prayed for" group. None of the patients, nurses, or attending physicians knew which group the patients were in.

Prayer groups around the nation were given only the first names, diagnoses, and prognoses of the first group of patients. They were asked to pray for each patient by name once each day. No other instructions were given.

The results were remarkable. The "prayed for" patients were five times less likely to require antibiotics and three times less prone to develop fluid filling their lungs. None of the prayed-for patients required breathing tubes, compared to twelve in the other group, and fewer of the prayed-for patients died during their treatment. The findings were published in the proceedings of the American Heart Association.

This study shows that at least one person in that prayer group was connecting with God, and that praying for others really can make a difference in improving people's health. Some people believe God healed people in biblical times but they're unsure if He still heals today. Yet the Scripture tells us, "Jesus Christ is the same yesterday, today, and forever" (Hebrews 13:8). Many people today testify that the Lord has miraculously healed them.

Duane Miller was pastor of First Baptist Church in Brenham, Texas. In 1990, he lost his voice due to a virus that infiltrated the nerves in his vocal chords. Medical experts said that this condition would leave him barely able to speak for the rest of his life. Even so, he continued to teach God's Word in a loud whisper to the best of his ability.

In 1993, he was miraculously healed as he was reading Psalm 103 to a church class. Amazingly, that teaching was recorded, which captured his vocal cords being healed as he read "He redeems my life from the pit." You can listen online to the actual recording of the moment he was healed.[21]

What does God's Word teach about healing? The Lord typically restores our health through the following avenues.

1. HEALING THROUGH DOCTORS AND SURGERY

God designed the human body to heal and repair itself to some degree. If you cut yourself in a minor way, you can put a bandage on it and your blood will clot. If you get a bruise, it will soon go away. But if you are seriously injured, break a bone, or have a heart attack, it goes without saying that you need to get to the hospital as quickly as possible.

Jesus said, "It is not those who are healthy who need a physician, but those who are sick" (Matthew 9:12). Luke, who wrote the books of Luke and Acts, was a physician (Colossians 4:14). If seeking treatment from a doctor is a lack of faith (as some people wrongly teach), Jesus would not have said this, and Luke would not have remained in his profession. It's terribly negligent to withhold medical care from your children or your loved ones because of your "faith." You can take them to get medical help and still pray for them to be healed. In fact, the work of doctors and nurses is one of the ways that God answers our prayers for healing.

As we grow older, our bodies weaken. The Scripture says, "When Isaac was old and his eyes were too dim to see . . ." (Genesis 27:1). Isaac was a man of faith but his eyesight worsened with his age. He needed glasses, but they hadn't been invented yet. Having some hearing aids might have helped too. Be thankful that the Lord has given us physicians, nurses, hospitals, and medical breakthroughs to bring healing to our bodies.

2. HEALING THROUGH MEDICINE

When Timothy was sick, Paul gave him this advice: "Don't continue drinking only water, but use a little wine because of your stomach and your frequent illnesses" (1 Timothy 5:23 HCSB). Timothy was frequently sick, so Paul recommended a little wine for medicinal purposes to heal his ailments. This would be similar to a doctor prescribing medicine to treat a sickness today. The Lord gives knowledge for the benefit of humankind, which includes providing scientific insights into how medicine can aid in curing sicknesses.

If God heals you through prayer, ask your doctor to confirm that you've been completely healed, and let him decide to take you off your medicine if you no longer need it. When Jesus healed the ten lepers, He told them to go to the temple priests who would inspect their bodies and pronounce them healed (Luke 10:14). Even if you are asking God to heal you, don't stop taking your prescribed medication, which could be a tragic mistake. If your condition is improving, your doctor will confirm it and will either lessen the dosage of your prescription or take you off it.

3. HEALING THROUGH PRAYER

God uses doctors and medicine to aid in healing, but sometimes neither is successful in treating the illness. In the New Testament, a woman had a hemorrhage for twelve years that couldn't be healed by doctors (Luke 8:43). In desperation, she came up behind Jesus and touched the hem of His robe—and immediately her bleeding stopped.

Although many people had been grabbing and touching Him, Jesus realized someone had touched Him in faith to receive healing because He knew that power had gone out from Him. Here we see an example of Jesus healing someone when physicians couldn't help.

The Lord wants us to seek Him for healing, even while we're receiving medical treatment. The Bible tells us, "In the thirty-ninth year of his reign Asa became diseased in his feet. His disease was severe, yet even in his disease he did not seek the LORD, but the physicians" (2 Chronicles 16:12). It wasn't wrong for Asa to ask help from physicians, but he didn't even consider the fact that God might want to heal him.

WHY ARE SOME PEOPLE NOT HEALED?

Why are some people healed while others are not? I cannot tell you why. Only the Lord knows. Jesus said, "There were many in Israel with leprosy in the time of Elisha the prophet, yet *not one of them was cleansed*—only Naaman the Syrian" (Luke 4:27 NIV). Naaman was healed. The other lepers were not.

I've known sick people who had great faith that they would be miraculously healed, but it didn't happen. And I've also known ill people who were very weak in faith, but they were healed. It doesn't make sense, but that hasn't stopped some people from giving their interpretation.

There are two theological extremes that offer explanations as to why someone isn't healed. One extreme view states, "You weren't healed because you didn't have enough faith." (But how do *you* know for sure how much faith a person has? Only God knows that.)

These people also believe that it's a lack of faith to even admit to being sick. But Jesus certainly didn't believe this, because He said, "It is not those who are healthy who need a physician, but those who are sick" (Mark 2:17). Jesus wants us to have compassion on those who are ill. He said, "I was sick, and you *visited* Me. . . . Truly I say to you, to the extent that you did it to one of these brothers of Mine, even the least of them, you did it to Me" (Matthew 25:36, 40).

The theological position on the other extreme teaches that no one can be miraculously healed today, regardless of their faith, because miraculous healing ceased when the apostles died. This teaching assumes that only the apostles could perform miracles, which isn't correct. God used Stephen, who was not one of the twelve, to perform miracles (Acts 6:8). Barnabas wasn't one of the twelve apostles either, but the Lord worked miracles through him and Paul (Acts 15:12).

People say, "You weren't healed because it wasn't God's will." (But how can you be so certain about what is *not* God's will?) Some people are more confident about what *isn't* God's will than they are about what is! It's easy to explain what you don't understand by saying, "It must not have been God's will for it to happen."

Neither of these two explanations is correct. Why some people aren't healed falls under the category of the "secret things" that belong to God (Deuteronomy 29:29). I've concluded that other unknown factors might be involved, which have nothing to do with faith or God's willingness to heal. There's a mystery in healing, which means we'll never figure out why not everyone has the same experience in this life. Just because some people are not healed doesn't cancel out the fact that many people have been miraculously cured—and that Jesus invites us to ask anything in His name.

Here are three different ways to pray for healing.

1. Ask God directly

The Lord invites you to come to Him in your time of need, which includes asking to be healed of your infirmities. "Let us therefore come boldly to the throne of grace, that we may obtain mercy and find grace to help in time of need" (Hebrews 4:16 NKJV). Don't tell yourself that you're not good enough to approach Him with your request. If you are a child of God, then He has given you His righteousness—and He invites you to "come *boldly* to His throne of grace." The Lord is not going to get upset with you for asking to be healed.

2. ASK OTHERS TO PRAY

Sometimes God wants to bring your healing through the prayers of others. The apostle James wrote, "Pray for one another so that you may be healed" (James 5:16).

In a church where I was pastor, a man named James trusted Jesus Christ to be his Lord and Savior. He mentioned to me one day that he had been dreaming the same nightmare every night for eight years. When he was a professional bodyguard eight years earlier, he fought and killed a man who tried to attack the client he was guarding.

Every night after this incident, James had the same agonizing nightmare of fighting with the man. This happened every night for eight years. In addition to this, he had insomnia, and every night it took him until at least 1 a.m. before he could fall asleep.

When I told James that I believed God wanted to set him free from the nightmare, he asked me to pray for him. As I prayed for his nightmare to leave in Jesus's name, he said, "I'm getting an excruciating headache." Then a few moments later he said, "I just felt something leave me," and immediately his head quit hurting.

He then became extremely sleepy and headed home to go to bed at 4 p.m. For the first time in eight years, he slept peacefully all night without dreaming of killing the man, and he never again had a problem with insomnia. This incident happened over a decade ago and his horrible nightmare has never returned.

Another member of our church who was a professional counselor heard his testimony about the recurring nightmare leaving through prayer. He told me, "We spend years counseling people who have recurring nightmares and cannot cure them. This proves that God can heal mental problems."

3. ASK THE ELDERS OF YOUR CHURCH TO PRAY

You can also be healed by requesting prayer from the leaders of your church. The Scripture says:

Is anyone among you sick? Then he must call for the elders of the church and they are to pray over him, anointing him with oil in the name of the Lord; and the prayer offered in faith will restore the one who is sick, and the Lord will raise him up, and if he has committed sins, they will be forgiven him. (James 5:14–15)

Why does James specifically tell us to ask for prayer from the elders? Although any believer can pray for someone else to be healed, asking the church leaders for prayer shows your willingness to submit to their authority. God's power flows down from heaven though His servants in the church. But the elders also have a responsibility—they must anoint those who are sick with oil in the name of Jesus, and pray in faith that the Lord will answer them. This isn't just a ritual prayer offered by those who aren't sure that God will heal. Those who are praying must truly believe that God hears their request and will answer it.

HEALING CAN TAKE PLACE INSTANTLY OR GRADUALLY

I've known people who were instantly healed of psychological issues like depression and physical problems through prayer. However, if you aren't instantly healed, don't assume that it will never happen. Normally, healing occurs gradually. Doctors do their best to treat their patients, but God is the one who brings restoration to the damaged area.

> If you aren't instantly healed, don't assume that it will never happen.

Often when our church prayer group has prayed for someone who is hospitalized, we've asked the Lord to speed up the patient's recovery. Many times we've seen patients healed more quickly than normal and released from the hospital earlier than expected.

Gradual healing is demonstrated by one of the miracles Christ performed. A blind man was brought to Him to have his eyes opened.

Jesus spat on his eyes, laid His hands on him, and asked, "Do you see anything?"

And he looked up and said, "I see men, for I see them like trees, walking around." *Then again He laid His hands on his eyes*; and he looked intently and was restored, and began to see everything clearly. (Mark 8:23–25)

In this incident, Jesus performed the healing as a process. First He opened the man's eyes so that he could see people with blurred vision. When He touched him a second time, he could see everything clearly. Jesus could have healed the man right away, but in this case He chose to lay His hands on the man twice. I believe Jesus purposefully performed this miracle in two stages to show that not all healings are instantaneous, but can also take place in stages of improvement.

One time a hard bump grew under my skin in the middle of my right hand, about the size of a marble cut in half. After it had been there for about six weeks, I thought, *This isn't going away and might require surgery to remove it.* I'll admit that I hadn't seriously asked God to heal me before then, so I finally prayed, "Lord, you created the universe and it's not too difficult for you to heal this little bump on my hand. I don't have the faith for it to instantly disappear, but I do believe that you can heal me gradually. I ask you to please heal my hand." This happened on a Thursday.

I don't remember even looking at my hand again until three days later. On Sunday morning, I looked at my hand and the bump was completely gone! I have no idea when it disappeared, other than that it happened sometime after I prayed on Thursday. The Lord answered my prayer, but the healing didn't take place the moment I prayed. This should encourage you to never give up when you don't see instantaneous results.

Every day we should be thanking God for our health or asking Him to heal us and our loved ones. Jesus healed ten lepers but only one thanked Him. I've heard far more people requesting healing than I have heard people thanking Him for their health. Don't forget to thank Him!

PRAYER

Heavenly Father, I realize that you are the same yesterday, today, and forever. You have the ability to heal my infirmity (*or name the person you are praying for*), and I ask you to have mercy on me (*or him/her*). I realize you that can heal in many ways, either instantly or gradually. I submit myself (*or name the person*) completely to you. Show me if I have any wrong attitude or if I am doing anything that's blocking my prayer from being answered. I trust your timing and thank you for hearing my prayer in Jesus' name.

25 | PRAYING FOR OTHERS

> "You also joining in helping us through
> your prayers." (2 Corinthians 1:11)

"Intercessory prayer" is prayer that asks God to do something for others. Perhaps the person you are praying for doesn't believe in Christ or is confused by false doctrines. Or maybe that person is addicted to drugs, or in intensive care at a hospital and barely hanging onto life. Although the situation may seem hopeless, your prayers can make a difference for people in trouble. The apostle Paul told the members of the church at Corinth that they were helping him through their prayers.

When the Israelites criticized God in the wilderness, the Lord sent poisonous snakes that bit many of the people. The disheartened Israelites came to Moses and said, "We have sinned, because we have spoken against the LORD and you; intercede with the LORD, that He may remove the serpents from us" (Numbers 21:7). Moses prayed on behalf of the people and God answered his request.

In another case, Moses' brother and sister slandered him:

> Then Miriam and Aaron spoke against Moses because of the Cushite woman whom he had married (for he had married a Cushite woman); and they said, "Has the LORD indeed spoken only through Moses? Has He not spoken through us as well?" And the LORD heard it. Now the man Moses was very humble, more than any man who was on the face of the earth. (Numbers 12:1–3)

The Lord was furious that Miriam and Aaron had opposed their brother, who was the most humble person on the planet, so He struck Miriam with leprosy. Aaron realized they had sinned and asked Moses to intercede for Miriam:

> Then Aaron said to Moses, "Oh, my lord, I beg you, do not account this sin to us, in which we have acted foolishly and in which we have sinned." . . . Moses cried out to the LORD, saying, "O God, heal her, I pray!" (Numbers 12:11, 13)

In both of these situations, the very people who slandered Moses came to him and asked for his prayers. Moses refused to be offended by their hypocrisy and called on the Lord to be merciful to them.

And the Lord also calls you to pray for the people who may have hurt you, including your enemies and those who don't hold the same beliefs or political views as you. When you intercede for them, you must lay aside your personal feelings and pray for them with a higher purpose. God listens to our intercessions for those who are in trouble or unable to pray for themselves.

> When you intercede for others, you must lay aside your personal feelings and pray with a higher purpose.

We've already discussed praying for your enemies and praying for others to be healed. Of course, we should also pray when others are going through a difficult situation, that God will provide what they need and will give wisdom about what to do. The Lord will listen to your passionate intercessions for them. Here are four more reasons to intercede for others.

Praying for a Lost Person's Soul to be Saved

Each person must individually choose to call upon the Lord to be saved, but your prayers can make it easier for others to respond to Him. Pray for the Holy Spirit to convict, indwell, and empower the people you are interceding for. First, pray that God would convict them of their sins. Then, pray for them to receive Jesus into their hearts. And finally, pray for the Holy Spirit to empower them to overcome sin.

1. Pray for God to open the lost person's heart.

Many people don't want anything to do with God because they have closed hearts. You cannot force a rosebud to open up. It must unfold from the inside. In the same way, the Lord can open a person's heart from the inside. The book of Acts tells us that while the apostle Paul was speaking to a group of women in Philippi, a certain woman—Lydia of Thyatira—was listening "and the *Lord opened her heart* to respond to the things spoken by Paul" (Acts 16:14).

Jesus said, "No one can come to Me unless the Father who sent Me draws him" (John 6:44). As you continue to intercede for unsaved people, the Lord convicts and persuades them to come to Him. The Holy Spirit works on their hearts in response to your prayers, which makes it easier for them to yield to God than to keep resisting Him.

> The Holy Spirit works on their hearts in response to your prayers, which makes it easier for them to yield to God than to keep resisting Him.

2. Pray for Lord to send others to share the gospel with the lost person.

Jesus said, "The harvest is abundant, but the workers are few. Therefore, *pray to the Lord of the harvest to send out workers* into His harvest" (Luke 10:2 HCSB). Many people assume He's talking about sending missionaries to foreign countries. But that's only a small part of what He meant. "The harvest" means everyone who needs to hear the message of salvation. Reaching the entire world with the gospel requires every believer to share Jesus and the good news of salvation with others.

When you ask God to send someone to share the gospel with an unsaved person, you're praying to "the Lord of the harvest to send out workers into His harvest." The laborer that God sends to speak to him or her could be a co-worker, a fellow student at school, or even a stranger.

Don't get discouraged if you don't see an immediate answer to your prayers. It could take years of praying before that lost person finally surrenders to the Lord, but your persistence will be worth the wait. Jesus told us to pray at all times and not lose heart (Luke 18:1).

James McConkey tells how George Müller had patiently prayed for five personal friends to be saved. After five years of praying, one came to Christ. Ten years later, two more were saved. He prayed for twenty-five years before the fourth man was saved. At the time of Müller's death, he had been praying for the fifth man for almost fifty-two years. This man came to Christ a few months after Müller died.[22]

I've prayed for years for certain people to be saved and I've seen them come to Jesus, one by one. Never give up interceding for others because you never know when the breakthrough might come.

Praying for Others to Change Their Behavior

How are you supposed to pray for a rebellious child, an estranged parent, or a wayward spouse? If you are interceding for a relative or close friend to change their behavior, you might have to endure their anger or mistreatment due to their resistance to God. As they fight against the conviction of the Holy Spirit, they will probably take out their frustrations on you.

A rebellious person is like a wild horse trying to throw off the rider who's trying to tame it. Bringing a person to repentance is a tumultuous process, and defiant people will keep bucking against

God until they finally submit. The Lord will give you the grace to endure their rude behavior if you will keep your hope fixed on Him.

When the prodigal son asked for his inheritance and left home for a foreign country, his father didn't chase him down the road begging him to come back (Luke 15:11–20). You cannot force someone to love you. As long as his heart was pointed away from home, he would never want to return. But if his heart could somehow turn around, then he would grow tired of rebelling and would want to go back home.

Here are two important things to pray for those who are in rebellion.

1. PRAY FOR THE HOLY SPIRIT TO CONVICT THEM OF THEIR SINS.

Newton's first law says that an object in motion will continue in the same direction unless it is acted upon by an external force. A rebellious person will continue down the wrong path unless God's holy presence convinces that individual to change course.

The only way anyone's heart can change is if the Holy Spirit opens their spiritual eyes to see the error of their ways. This is why it's so important for us to intercede for those who are heading down the road of destruction. The Lord will respond to our pleas by convicting them of their sins and their need to repent (John 16:8).

2. PRAY FOR THEM TO BECOME MISERABLE IN THEIR LIFESTYLE.

Why would anyone want to change if they enjoy what they're doing? They won't. The circumstances surrounding the person you are praying for will need to get worse before they will get better. It's for this reason you must pray that the defiant person will get so fed up with his ungodly way of life that he will never want to return to it. Genuine sorrow will turn a person's heart around. "For the sorrow that is according to the will of God produces a repentance without regret, leading to salvation" (2 Corinthians 7:10).

After the prodigal son left home he wasted his money on loose living. He probably enjoyed his rebellion at first, but then the party came to an abrupt halt when he ran out of money and a famine hit. It wasn't until he was eating husks in a pigpen that he came to his senses (Luke 15:17). When he hit bottom, it finally dawned on him that he had been much happier at home. He got up out of the pigpen and returned home with a totally different attitude.

If you are enjoying seeing the rebellious person you're praying for become miserable, something is terribly wrong with your attitude. The purpose of intercession is to bring about life-change in someone, not vengeance. As you continue to pray, the rebellious person may come to the point when he cannot stand what he is doing. He may become so miserable that it's easier for him to surrender to the Lord than to continue in rebellion. God won't take away his free will, but your prayers of intercession can strongly influence the person to repent.

Paul had an interesting way of praying for rebellious people. He writes that he turned an unrepentant man in the Corinthian church over to the devil: "I have decided to *deliver such a one to Satan* for the destruction of his flesh, so that his spirit may be saved in the day of the Lord Jesus" (1 Corinthians 5:5). In this verse, *flesh* means "sinful desires." Paul wasn't praying for this rebellious man to die, but for his selfish attitude to be destroyed. Since the man wouldn't listen to correction, Satan was permitted to intensify his attacks on him, which caused him to repent of his sin (2 Corinthians 2:6–8).

He also writes that he used the same tactic for two other troublemakers: "Hymenaeus and Alexander, whom I have *handed over to Satan*, so that they will be taught not to blaspheme" (1 Timothy 1:20). This doesn't mean he wanted them to go to hell, but that the Lord would remove His blessing and hedge of protection for a short time (see Job 1:9–12). By doing this, they would suffer such anguish that they would stop blaspheming.

Some people only learn the hard way. They have to hit bottom like the prodigal son before they will come to their senses.

Praying for Those in Authority

"First of all, then, I urge that entreaties and prayers, petitions and thanksgivings, be made on behalf of all men, for kings and all who are in authority, so that we may lead a tranquil and quiet life in all godliness and dignity" (1 Timothy 2:1–2). "All who are in authority" means government leaders including the president, Congress, the Supreme Court, governors, mayors, and police officers. It also includes our pastors, employers, supervisors, and school teachers. Their decisions can make our lives easier or more difficult, but we have a secret weapon called intercession, through which the Lord can move their thoughts in the right direction.

God has the power to change minds. "The LORD can control a king's mind as he controls a river; he can direct it as he pleases" (Proverbs 21:1 NCV). He can inject thoughts into the leaders' minds to make decisions they normally wouldn't make.

As you intercede for those in authority over you, God can give you favor in their eyes so they will be supportive of you rather than fight against you. "When a man's ways are pleasing to the LORD, He makes even his enemies to be at peace with him" (Proverbs 16:7). Your intercession will result in a more peaceful life for you, so you can enjoy "a tranquil and quiet life in all godliness and dignity."

When you "find favor" with others they will do you *favors* because you are their *favorite* person. Joseph in the Old Testament "found favor" with Potiphar, who promoted him to a higher position (Genesis 39:4). And even if the authorities you are praying for don't change their minds, the Lord will bless you with peace simply because you obeyed His instructions to pray for them. When I intercede for those in authority, I pray for their relationship with God and for their salvation. If they will submit to the Lord, then He can show them how to make wise decisions. I will also pray for the specific issue that concerns me. I ask God to influence that person's heart so they will do what is right. However, if we don't intercede for our leaders, the Lord may keep His hands off the situation and we may suffer the consequences.

PRAYING FOR FUTURE GENERATIONS

I believe one of the most overlooked intercessions is to pray every day for our children, grandchildren, and even those descendants who are yet to be born.

God told Abraham to look at the stars to get a glimpse of the future generations of his descendants. "Now look toward the heavens, and count the stars, if you are able to count them." And He said to him, "So shall your descendants be" (Genesis 15:5). Another time, God told Abraham, "I will surely bless you and make your descendants as numerous as the stars in the sky and as the sand on the seashore" (Genesis 22:17).

The Lord wants us to be concerned about the spiritual welfare of our future descendants. For example, the following passage from Psalms refers to four successive generations, including "the children yet to be born."

> For He established a testimony in Jacob and appointed a law in Israel, which He commanded our fathers [*generation #1*] that they should teach them to their children [*generation #2*], that the generation to come might know, even the *children yet to be born* [*generation #3*], that they may arise and tell them to their children [*generation #4*] that they should put their confidence in God and not forget the works of God, but keep His commandments. (Psalm 78:5–7)

What should you pray for your children and those yet to be born? Ask that the Holy Spirit will work in their hearts so they'll be saved, even at a young age. Ask the Lord to protect and bless them, to keep them morally pure, and that they will always live to please Him. You should also pray for their future families that they will be saved and have a close walk with God.

Since God isn't bound by time and exists in tomorrow, it's no problem for Him to remember your prayers until the time your future descendants are born. He can cause them to walk on the correct path in answer to your prayers. We know that Timothy was influenced by the prayers of his grandmother. Paul wrote: "I am reminded of your sincere faith, *which first lived in your grandmother* Lois and in your mother Eunice and, I am persuaded, now lives in you also" (2 Timothy 1:5 NIV).

So don't give up praying. You have no idea how your prayers are making a difference, both now and in the years to come.

NOTES

1. Marv Hinten, "Monkey Pray, Monkey Get," *Light & Life*, March/April 2004.

2. Kent Crockett, *Making Today Count for Eternity* (Sisters, OR: Multnomah, 2001), p. 60.

3. Kent Crockett, *The Sure Cure for Worry* (Minneapolis: Chosen, 2013), p. 218.

4. *Beaumont Examiner,* March 26, 1998.

5. You can find a detailed study of fulfilled Bible prophecies in my book *The Sure Cure for Worry* (Minneapolis: Chosen, 2013), chapter 3, "Indisputable Proof God Controls the World."

6. G. Bertram, "*thauma, thaumazo, thaumasios, thaumastos,*" in *Theological Dictionary of the New Testament, Abridged in One Volume,* Geoffroy W. Bromiley, ed. Gerhard Kittel and Gerhard Friederich (Grand Rapids: Eerdmans, 1985), p. 317.

7. Kent Crockett, *The Sure Cure for Worry* (Minneapolis: Chosen, 2013), pp. 177–78.

8. For more information about finding the right person to marry, see my book *The Sure Cure for Worry* (Minneapolis: Chosen Books, 2013), chapter 13, "Trusting God to Provide."

9. John F. Walvoord and Roy B. Zuck, eds., *The Bible Knowledge Commentary: Old Testament* (Wheaton, IL: Victor, 1985), p. 1367.

10. Texas Baptist Leadership, 1995.

11. William Barclay, *The Revelation of John,* vol. 2 (Philadelphia: Westminster John Knox, 1976), p. 41.

12. John F. Walvoord, *The Revelation of Jesus Christ* (Chicago: Moody, 1966), p. 152.

13. Peter Lord, *Hearing God* (Grand Rapids: Chosen, 2011), p. 73.

14. *Leadership,* Spring 1995, p. 49.

15. Malcolm Smith, *Jesus and the Pharisees,* lecture series, Unconditional Love International, 1975, compact disc.

16. Compiled from the Associated Press report, March 6, 2002, and other eye-witness reports.

17. Henry G. Bosch, "The Power of Prayer," *Our Daily Bread* (Grand Rapids: Radio Bible Class Ministries), April 5, 2000, http://odb.org/2000/04/05/the-power-of-prayer/.

18. Kent Crockett, *The Sure Cure for Worry* (Minneapolis: Chosen, 2013), p. 95.

19. Kent Crockett, *Slaying Your Giants* (Peabody, MA: Hendrickson, 2013), p. 7.

20. Brian Bauknight, *The Brain-Mind Bulletin*, No. 7, March 24, 1986, and the *Chicago Sun-Times*.

21. To see the video, go to www.youtube.com and search for "Duane Miller video by Crossroads Church Media." The direct link to the YouTube video is https://www.youtube.com/watch?v=NuBV3uPxaAc. For more on Duane Miller, see www.nuvoice.org.

22. Recounted in DeVern Fromke, *Life's Ultimate Privilege* (Cloverdale, IN: Sure Foundation, Inc., 1986), Day 2, p. 8.